Heartland

Also by Mark C. Scott

Reinspiring the Corporation: the seven seminal paths to corporate greatness

The Professional Service Firm: a manager's guide to maximising profit and value

Value Drivers: the manager's guide to driving corporate value creation

All published by John Wiley & Sons.

Heartland

*How to Build Companies
as Strong as Countries*

Mark C. Scott

John Wiley & Sons, Ltd

Chichester · New York · Weinheim · Brisbane · Singapore · Toronto

Other Wiley Editorial Offices

John Wiley & Sons, Inc., 605 Third Avenue,
New York, NY 10158-0012, USA

Wiley-VCH GmbH, Pappelallee 3,
D-69469 Weinheim, Germany

John Wiley & Sons Australia Ltd, 33 Park Road, Milton,
Queensland 4064, Australia

John Wiley & Sons (Asia) Pte Ltd, 2 Clementi Loop #02–01,
Jin Xing Distripark, Singapore 129809

John Wiley & Sons (Canada) Ltd, 22 Worcester Road,
Rexdale, Ontario M9W 1L1, Canada

British Library Cataloguing in Publication Data
A catalogue record for this book is available from the British Library

ISBN 0-471-49936-6

Typeset in Goudy 12/15 pt by Florence Production Ltd, Stoodleigh, Devon
Printed and bound in Great Britain by Biddles Ltd, Guildford and King's Lynn

This book is printed on acid-free paper responsibly manufactured from
sustainable forestry, in which at least two trees are planted for each one used for
paper production.

In fond memory of Ellen Gadiel,
Kenneth Scott and Marjorie Korn

Contents

Preface
A map of the human heart

In that seminal moment in Joseph Conrad's *Heart of Darkness*, Kurtz – the archetypal lost soul – screams out in the blackness of the night, 'The horror! The horror!' Kurtz's half-maddened soliloquy in the dark heart of the Congo resonates for us all. When all the commotion stops, when the phone falls silent, when the memory of all those precious moments is rekindled, we all grasp for something more permanent to cling to, some identity to save us from the quicksands of futility and irrelevance.

The fundamental source of solace, of meaning, in most of our lives is to be found in each other – through our family, our friendships and through participation in a wider community often defined by ethnicity. Without participation in a community of some sort, meaning quickly drains away.

Meaning is in a social construct. Few of us can survive like anchorites in our monastic cells. Our lives are governed by maps of relationships. We even write them into our Palm Pilots. They make the physical environment in which we exist meaningful. They define how we interact with objective reality. Without our social maps we are literally lost souls. Our greatest fear is exclusion, a fear first born in the school yard. Joseph Conrad caught the phobia exquisitely in the uncharted interior of the black continent where Kurtz loses his mind. To be mapless is to be literally lost.

Our working lives are no different. Our place of work is a social environment where success is the product of our dealings with other people, whether our boss, our clients or our suppliers. Companies are social units, with the same human lifeblood as any other types of social construct. But that is not how we usually understand them. Instead of maps of relationships, the primary coordinates we typically use to understand businesses are financial ratios. Their North is earnings per share; their East is revenue growth; their South is pre-tax margin; their West is return on capital employed. Our maps of companies are drawn up by financial analysts, largely for the benefit of investors. Management has evolved over the last thirty years to the status of a pseudo-science. As with all sciences, the emphasis is on measurement. The metrics have evolved. The latest are total shareholder returns and EVA. But, essentially, the map is one based on quantification of good old solid assets.

Is this map the one that really matters? It clearly plays its role in determining output, but should we see the world of the corporation solely in that dimension? If we see the corporation solely as a desiccated landscape of assets, then yes, the traditional lens of financial measurement is probably appropriate. But, if we understand it as more than that, that indeed the landscape of the firm is more about people and relationships than assets, then we need a new sort of map.

For the past twenty years, since the publication of Michael Porter's hugely influential *Competitive Advantage*, the corporate landscape has been dominated by concerns about capital and assets. Manufacturing-oriented business was in the driving seat and what mattered was competitive positioning and productivity. Things have now changed. Services account for almost 50 per cent of output and professional services, as a subset, account for 7 per cent of output. Even manufacturing firms are morphing into consulting firms. Eighty per cent of manufacturing value added comes from intangibles.

In a market of cost parity, competitive advantage is now a differentiation game. The driver of differentiation is talent. We have gone from cash to flesh and blood as the primary source of competitive advantage. With it, most of the paradigms we have followed for the past three decades should fall away, as we move from asset issues to people issues. But that is not what has happened. On the whole, our understanding of business is still based on assets. We measure output as if the company were a machine with all the associated predictability. It is not.

If the prime source of competitive advantage for firms is people, the most pressing issue is social management. We need to understand the business as a social phenomenon. That means we need new maps. We need a map of the society of the corporation – of its villages, its towns, its trade links, its communicational infrastructure, its philosophy and beliefs. In short, we need a map that tells us how the corporation functions as a social unit. We need a map of its heartland. The question is where do we find the blueprint?

In the precursive book to this one, *Reinspiring the Corporation*, we suggested one place to turn for examples of social maps was the world's great religious movements. The seven great religious movements – Hinduism, Christianity, Buddhism, Confucianism, Islam, Judaism and Taoism – have all survived essentially whole for over a thousand years, twenty times the length of the average corporation. They count in their number three-quarters of the world's population and define the values underlying almost all national societies. They are a seminal dimension of the social map of the world.

We educed that their competitive advantage as global social units was based on core building blocks which are common to them all – a strong framework of moral governance where individual priorities are satisfied through group objectives, a unifying and unique shared language where a fabric of stories keeps the flame of heritage alive, an intense exchange of ideas and dialogue, but always within a context of positive ambition for self-betterment, and an acute sense that membership of the community confers a status no-one would willingly forgo. We proposed that the same characteristics could be readily co-opted by firms wishing to develop cohesive societies capable of delivering long-term competitive advantage.

There was one inevitable weakness in using religious organisation as an analogy for business. The underlying aspect of belief and spirituality is clearly absent from the communities of companies. So we posed ourselves the question, what other institutions could offer a model for how to create competitive social units? On reflection one didn't have to look very far. The social unit that dominates our lives, and indeed dominates the geopolitical balance of world power, is of course the Nation State. It provides our sense of identity and preserves our social functionality. Our lives and even our characters are defined by the heartland of the Nation State.

The Nation State is founded on a highly-evolved political process and hence is much more overt in its management philosophy than the great religions. The Nation State is physically defined. It possesses laws, it exercises fiscal authority. Religion is no longer active in this secular form except for in anomalous instances such as Israel or Bhutan. But does the Nation State provide important lessons about how to manage social relationships and can these lessons be co-opted successfully by firms?

This book proposes that there is a core set of characteristics that forms the heartland of any social organisation. These characteristics are replicated almost exactly in both the great religions and the Nation State – the two largest and most potent social structures civilisation has ever produced. This book also posits that they can be applied to the company – only no strategist has yet done so.

We stand at a point in time where companies never appear to have had more potential to dominate the workings of the planet. They are larger than ever before. They are more global than ever before. Their rates of productivity have never been matched. Their current market value could never before have been dreamt of. They dominate world trade and world trade dwarfs the GNP of Nation States. But, paradoxically, they have also never been weaker. In 1900, the traffic in London moved at an average speed of around ten miles an hour and, despite all the advancements, that is precisely where it stands today. For the company the story is no different. The average lifespan of the large firm stands at 38 years, marginally less than the average a century ago. This is not for lack of trying. Most firms have aggressively tackled the twin issues of unit costs and productivity. Faced with relentless competitive strain on margins, firms have never been under greater pressure to differentiate. They are also under acute duress to do so on a global basis. The question they all face is where can they find new sources of competitive advantage? Where can they find the elixir of corporate life?

Few firms have yet acknowledged that competitive advantage is fundamentally dependent on understanding and managing their own social dynamics. The only strategy that is genuinely long term is social strategy. Get that wrong and the seeds of the firm's destruction are already sown. The firm must respond to the seminal cry in the heart of every employee, 'why am I doing this?' If it cannot, it is irrelevant to all of us lost in our personal Kurtzian jungles.

1

The ambivalent corporation: global giant or house of straw?

In October 1982 an aquiline, aristocratic-faced man sat at his desk in his well-appointed seventeenth-floor office in Atlanta, Georgia. Roberto Goizueta had fled Cuba in 1960 amid the whirlwind of Castro's revolution. He had lost every cent of his inheritance and arrived in America penniless. He was now 49, in his prime, and CEO of Coca-Cola. He had seen the world and assessed its opportunities. Twenty thousand employees answered to him and his firm controlled approximately 50 per cent of the domestic soft drinks market. That wild young immigrant of yore had plenty of reason to be proud of his achievements. The American dream was his.

But as Goizueta sat at his desk, a deep frown etched his brow. There was a nagging doubt in his mind that such feelings of self-congratulation were premature. Roberto Goizueta was smart enough to appreciate that domestic dominance was not enough. The game was subtly shifting. There was a prize bigger than the US. The only market that mattered in the long run was the world.

It was shortly thereafter that Goizueta hatched his grand vision. It was exhilarating in its simplicity – to get a Coke within hand reach of every soul on earth. He had seen enough of far-flung places to appreciate the vast gulf separating distinct cultures and ethnic tastes. But he still held on to the almost evangelistic conviction that, if Coke could induce such loyalty amongst his fellow American citizens, then it could do the same with the rest of humanity. The challenge was to build an organisation with sufficient reach to get the product to all these disparate markets, to carry the message into every corner of the planet. If he was to leave Coke with anything, it would be with that vision of global dominance etched on the minds of every manager the firm employed.

Few people remember the name Goizueta. But everyone subscribes to his vision. Goizueta's dream has become the precept underlying the corporate strategy of most large firms today. Since the late 1980s firms have expanded globally in a way not witnessed since the heyday of the Dutch East India Company in the 1750s and the expansion of the imperial European powers in the 1800s. It is no longer viable to be a national champion alone.

This sea change has meant a dramatic shift in the stature of the company. If the twentieth century was the age of the Nation State, it will become increasingly tempting to call the twenty-first century the age of the corporation. For most of the twentieth century world economics were dictated by the relative positions of the great powers. Economics was clearly subordinated to politics. From the First World War in

1914 to the Second World War in 1939, and even well into the cold war, the tools and mechanisms of commerce were directly subordinate to furthering the political objectives of rival states.

Ten years on from the fall of the Berlin Wall, things have all the appearances of a dramatic alteration. Economics and not politics drives the wealth of regions. Wealth, not geopolitical influence, is the Holy Grail. And the economic levers are no longer the exclusive property of the state. World economic activity is dominated by large firms. Microsoft, despite the threat of dismemberment, rivals the GNP of Spain with a market cap of $600 billion. Hewlett Packard's worth rivals that of Greece. IBM's at $200 billion approximately equates to that of Colombia. Lucent weighs in next to South Africa. Already, 46 out of the top 100 economies are companies not countries and it is still early days in the great game of globalisation. And their power has been gathering at startling speed. The revenue of the top ten industrial companies has been growing at twice the average rate of GDP growth for the major economies.

Global consolidation of major firms is continuing to create new giants to rival the productive capacity of Nation States. The assets of the ten largest banks have doubled every five years for the past thirty years – twice the rate of growth of the banking industry in general. It does not take much imagination to picture the relative power of such firms versus countries when, over the next decade, global consolidation will probably distil the auto industry down to four major enterprises, the telco sector down to three key players, the airline industry down to four networks and media down to half a dozen enterprises, each cabal controlling 50 per cent of their respective industries. Firms are merging to form global leviathans faster than countries can hold summits to harmonise trade. The rate of annual M&A hit $2 trillion in 1999. The mergers are too numerous to itemise – from Chase/Chemical Bank, CibaGeigy/Santos, BP/Amoco, Travelers/Citigroup, AOL/Time Warner, to Vodafone/ Mannesmann. The list is staggering.

The lifeblood of this new global world is trade. Trade is vast and trade is between companies, not countries. Daily global trade is equivalent to the annual GDP of Germany. Daily currency trading exceeds transaction in physical goods and services by a factor of ten. As countries struggle to manage their budgets, balance their trade, and maintain their currencies, the very tool they have to play with – international commerce – is no longer under their control. And the virtual global market, the World Wide Web, which no country controls and which may ultimately rival its real counterpart, is only in its infancy.

A small assembly of globally competitive corporations accounts for the bulk of world trade. The activities of only 20 companies, for example, account for 50 per cent of Japanese exports to the US, and the activities of 50 companies for 75 per cent of exports. For such firms national politics is increasingly an irritation salved by employing a hot government relations consultancy. Global firms are the Tyrannosaurus Rexes in the commercial jungle of the world marketplace.

Do corporations really rule the earth?

It is this vision of the omnipotent corporation that has so fed the popular imagination. Orwell's 'Big Brother' is a Monsanto feeding the world genetically warped corn that could kill every form of hedgerow life the world possesses. But has the era of the corporate world really arrived? Are firms destined to inherit the earth? Has economics finally vanquished politics? Is Goizueta's dream close to consummation? If you subscribe to the prognostications of the gurus of global trade, such as Kenichi Omae or George Soros, the answer would be yes. But the fact is that things are not so clear cut. The statistics of size and growth of trade stand in stark contrast to the bio-signs of even the largest companies.

For all the talk of size and might, most companies remain intensely fragile and ephemeral. Even very large companies rarely survive longer than a modest human career – around forty years. Firms have never been richer and never more global in operation, but they show no signs of enhancing their longevity. Their biological success is very limited. The question that everyone in business should therefore be asking is why? Such frailty at a time of such apparent strength is a bizarre paradox.

The usual stock-in-trade explanations for the short life of the average corporation boil down to a criticism of excessive short-termism. It is certainly the case that, ironically enough, global competition appears to be intensifying this spiral of short-termism. As competition intensifies and investors get more demanding, the pressure to focus on hand-to-mouth survival has never been greater. Quarterly EPS targets dominate the corporate agenda. So-called corporate strategy has, for sure, been excessively focused for the past decade on quick margin-enhancement gizmos such as reengineering. The average tenure of the CEO is now down to four years, so what else would you expect?

But this does not explain what appears to be a more profound and structural fallibility on the part of large firms. The possibility that there exists some other fatal flaw must be taken seriously, particularly given the fact that the global playing-field now appears to be so heavily slanted in favour of the firm. What is it about the firm that makes it such a fragile locus of creativity despite its apparent strength? This is a question with vast ramifications, but one thing is clear: large firms are in a tough spot despite their apparent hegemony.

The roots of corporate frailty

Let us reflect for a moment on the nature of the modern corporation. Major firms have traditionally been characterised by a concentration of productive capacity and capital necessary to sustain it. What mattered was sustaining utilisation, productivity and competitive costs. As we all know, things have progressively changed since 1970. A single-mindedly manufacturing and cost management orientation is no longer a source of decisive competitive advantage for most large Western firms. On average only 35 per cent of value added is generated in manufacturing. The rest arises through intangibles such as branding, marketing and various aspects of service. Whilst such intangibles have a capital requirement, capital is not the lifeblood of the modern value chain. The essential ingredient to an intangibles-based value chain is people. Competitiveness and innovation are a direct corollary of a firm's ability to attract, retain and manage talent. The shift from capital to grey matter is probably the single biggest economic transition since 1850, and far more seminal than the advent of IT per se.

Given that modern companies are nothing other than collections of talented people, it is worth considering how the company is a reflection of more fundamental human

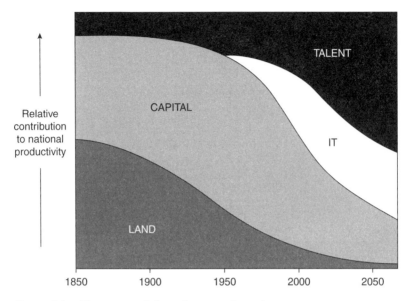

Figure 1.1   Illustrative shift in factors of production

principles. People naturally form associations called societies. It is this social phenomenon, on such a large and organised scale, that differentiates us humans most from other forms of life on earth. Societies have rules and evolve methodologies for self-governance. The fundamental process of managing societies is called politics. Without participation in such a society we as individuals are deracinated, outcasts, and as such quickly suffer an erosion of personal identity. None of us are islands unto ourselves. The society with which we choose to identify most closely will, of course, vary. Indeed, over the passage of time the types of communities that have meaning to us also vary. But there is one constant – that impulse to social inclusion and recognition is what drives us all.

The dominant units of social organisation that dictate most of our lives are not companies of course, they are countries.

Most of us have an intimate association with our place of upbringing, with our heartland. We closely identify with the cultural and ethical foundations of our nation of birth. Most of the fabric of our lives is fundamentally local in nature, through from an affinity for a certain cut of hedgerow to familiarity with the quirky configuration of convenience stores. We gain reassurance from an understanding of the legal and moral framework that prevails and derive fundamental security from the state subsidy of pensions and healthcare.

This quality of localness also pervades our consumption habits. In most countries the mass market shows keen preference for locally produced goods. In fact, what any country

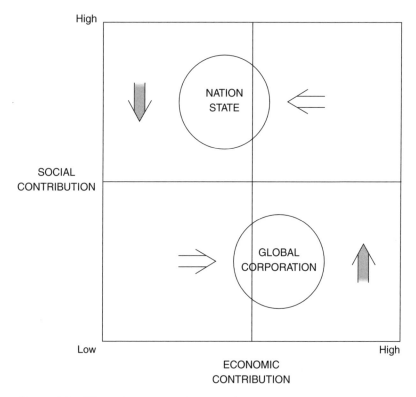

Figure 1.2   The relative contribution of companies versus countries

consumes is typically 90 per cent produced within its borders. Americans will probably never stomach Marmite on their toast and Brits will probably never understand the predilection for putting ice instead of milk in tea! For these associated reasons, few of us would contemplate moving countries permanently for work. It is much more likely that we would move employers.

We have talked of the apparent might of large corporates dwarfing their national hosts in economic terms. However, in social terms the position of companies and countries is reversed. Companies are comparatively weak. Critically, in a social sense most corporations are not as global as they would like to think. They are largely tied to the Nation State. Like people, and precisely because they are made up of people, they tend collectively to derive their strength from their national origins. Whilst they can have the appearance of being global economically, in a social sense they have not evolved away from their national heartland.

The not so global firm

In an age of global markets, one would assume that both debt and equity are now nationless. Firms can raise either anywhere to fuel operations anywhere else. In reality, however, the majority of larger firms derive their capital base from their home market where they are quoted. In the case of US firms it is rare that major corporations are even listed outside the NYSE or Nasdaq. The majority raise all their debt from indigenous sources. Key shareholders are dominantly US institutions with long-term relationships. In the case of Japan the nationalism of capital is even more extreme. Whilst, for example, 60 per cent of Honda's sales are outside Japan, only

10 per cent of its stock is held by non-Japanese. It is still comparatively rare for a German firm to raise debt in the Euro markets. Perhaps one exception to the rule is, oddly enough, the British firm. Although their main listing will typically be on the LSE, they often have parallel ADRs or ADSs quoted in the US. It is their only way of tapping into US institutions which deal primarily in US securities. That is a compelling motive to cross the Pond!

Whilst the growth in mutual funds has facilitated foreign ownership of stocks, the penetration of global holdings in indigenous funds is still low. The large mutual funds such as Fidelity, Wells Fargo, and Calpers with $2 trillion under management, usually invest no more than 10 per cent of their portfolios overseas. If Mexico or Indonesia goes soft, they will typically rein back on all their overseas investments. Foreign is foreign after all!

But it is in the fabric of management rather than capital that nationalism has its strongest hand. The average corporate employs a majority of nationals amongst its senior ranks. The CEO slot is almost universally reserved for a national. Only about 10 per cent of the board seats of public US corporations are held by non-US nationals. Only one in five US corporate boards even include a non-US citizen. And of the non-US nationals on US boards, 40 per cent are either British or Canadian. In other words, they share common Anglo-Saxon roots and an ardent love of the Queen! The tally of foreign board representation in Japanese, German and French corporations is, not surprisingly, even sparser.

So what does this mean for the corporate dream of globalism, for the virile, macho, world-dominating corporation? There are some high-profile cases of global corporations flexing their muscles with foreign governments. And it is these that colour the popular imagination about the brute, bullying, union-bashing corporate. Such episodes usually centre on the level of government subsidy available to underwrite new operations. BMW prominently threatened to abandon its investment in the Longbridge manufacturing unit of Rover, a mainstay of employment in the midlands of England, until Tony Blair's government acquiesced with a tax break of £140 million. Eighteen months later it pulled out regardless.

However, despite their gathering power, corporations do not appear to have significant leverage over the national markets in which they compete. The corporation as a social unit is firmly subordinate to the Nation State. If anything, most firms are trying to reaccommodate themselves with, rather than dominate, the state. Three years on from Roberto Goizueta's death, Coca-Cola has publicly humbled itself in espousing a new market-sensitive stance, abandoning (at least purportedly!) its one-world imperialism. P&G, that paragon of global centrism, extraordinarily appears to be doing the same.

The way of all flesh and blood

The Achilles' heel of the global corporate dream is people. In our MBA era, where global educational standards abound, it is commonly supposed that skilled labour is mobile; that a talented consultant or programmer from London can readily relocate to Silicon Valley if the pay is right; that the Nation State is no longer a constraint to the mobility of talent; that large companies might choose to deploy such talent anywhere globally anytime; that they control their human resources much as they do their capital.

This is simply not so. The loyalty of most employees is to the community of the state they live in. The lives of most are indelibly and umbilically connected to the countries

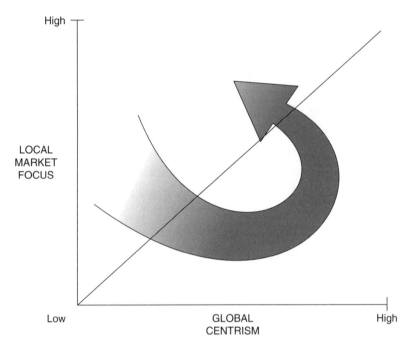

Figure 1.3   The evolution of corporate strategy

they inhabit. It is a minority that are able and willing to follow the global career opportunities of a global employer. The expatriate life is still limited to a small group of senior executives and they too are increasingly less willing to sacrifice the bonds of local community for the lure of the corporate career. Corporations therefore compete for a talent base whose principal loyalty is to location and nation, not to a company.

That also means corporates have less leverage with governments than might be supposed. Most national employment is created by small and medium-size enterprises, typically selling to the local market. It is these businesses that keep governments in power, not the prosperity of global corporations. As recently as ten years ago, governments were still prioritising the patronage and championing of big national businesses, from airlines to steel. Those days are largely gone. Even xenophobic corporate Germany acquiesced to the hostile acquisition of Mannesman by Vodafone. Instead the contemporary mission of most Western governments is where it probably should be – the defence of the welfare of its voting population. Safeguarding employment remains the mission, irrespective of the nationality of the employer. Although corporate competitiveness is no longer the property of the Nation State, what is effectively property of the Nation State are the factor resources – educated people. The Nation State has the fundamental role to play in the process of achieving social cohesion.

Governments are also under increasing pressure to provide their citizens with open access to the best and cheapest goods and services available. Fifteen years ago many fought to sustain national champions by ensuring them a captive consumer market. Outside France that strategy is now defunct, and even in France the Internet will play its role in eroding dirigism. The proposed dismemberment of Microsoft by the US courts illustrates the seriousness with which Washington takes its guardianship of consumer interests. The forced opening up of car distribution in the UK heralds a similar prerogative. Interestingly, governments are increasingly put in the position of policing corporations in local markets in the interests of their local customers.

This national role of defender of local consumer interest is all the more potent because of the resolute endurance of local tastes. Kenichi Ohmae, like many others, has argued vehemently that the Californianisation of tastes means that homogeneous offerings can be shipped globally across all sectors. Outside certain categories such as software and

medical instruments, all of which tend to have a high technological component, most products and services are
fundamentally national in nature. And even if a core product
is global, it is likely that the bulk of value added will lie in
marketing and service, both of which are intrinsically local.
The ritualised nature of shopping makes it typically a local
phenomenon. Even Web players like Yahoo and Amazon
localise their national sites. In such a situation global scale
becomes less relevant than national scale and national market
share. The relevant competitive unit is still the Nation State
– as Coke itself admitted in its crestfallen avowal to adapt
to local needs with more sensitivity.

The dominant influence over the behaviour of both
consumers and employees is therefore the political process of
local government. It is politics, not economics, which conditions the behaviour of most people, both as employees and
as consumers. It is the electorate and not shareholders to
whom the dominant drivers of society are answerable.

Life between a rock and an ever harder place

If on the one hand the Nation State exerts overwhelming trac-
tion over the human constituents of companies, corporations
are becoming equally disempowered by their non-human
lifeblood – capital. Whilst it is still the case that the majority
of a corporation's capital will be raised in its home market,
the capital markets themselves are global. The capital system
is like the human circulatory system, with cash being pumped
out to the peripheral economies from the core markets of
Western Europe and the US, only to be washed back in from
the periphery to the financial centres for recirculation. Capital

markets are much more truly global than companies. Money is quite literally allocated to areas of highest return. Portfolios of risk are managed on a global basis from the large number of dealing rooms around the major cities. Capital has no political allegiance. It knows no nationality. It has no personality. It has no fixed assets to uproot. Unlike the corporation it can relocate in days or even hours.

This being the case, the so-called global firm, far from approaching its apotheosis, is increasingly in an invidious position. On one side it is inexorably linked to the individual political processes of each market in which it competes. Unless it can play each country's game it will neither have committed employees nor loyal customers. It is almost certainly, if unconsciously, for this reason that even the largest firms tend still to be fundamentally wedded to their home markets where they can achieve competitive advantage on both scores. It is also for this reason that in excess of 60 per cent of the world's global firms are either American or Japanese, as both enjoy a huge home market.

On the other side of the equation, the corporation is increasingly having to compete for global, free-flowing capital which is entirely fickle and transactional. It obeys an ever-shifting pattern driven largely by perceptions of local political market outcomes. Again, the firm's surest route to competitive advantage is to root its capital structure in its home market where strength of relationships with institutions can obviate the need to compete for more global capital.

Emperor's New Clothes syndrome

The so-called global firm is not therefore really global in any sense other than it operates in multiple countries. It does not employ global people in its key decision-making roles, it does not compete for global consumers (if such people really exist!) as core loyalists and it does not participate in the global capital process other than inadvertently. Most importantly, it cannot compete with the national heartland for the loyalty of its employees. Nor can it really claim to represent itself as the arbiter of customer interests.

Given this subordination of the firm to larger political and social systems, it should not be surprising that the average firm only endures forty years. It has no real, lasting social purpose. It is only entities with real social and political purpose that endure. The only purpose of the average firm is to produce wealth for shareholders; shareholders whose wealth is readily migrant and who can invest in infinite places. Such a purely economic goal makes the corporation transitory.

Arie de Geus has argued eloquently that the company be construed as a living, social organism.[1] However, the organic analogy is not borne out in the case of most companies. We as individual organisms certainly live to profit, and to enjoy the fruits of our profit. But we are also driven by something more fundamental – the urge to expand, propagate and grow in all senses, both physically, intellectually and spiritually. This impulse of individuals to reproduce and expand is magnified when we form societies to protect and promote our interests. Societies, particularly based on ethnic roots, demonstrate a passionate urge to expand.

It is this organic urge to achieve enlargement, and thereby at least the illusion of immortality, that modern corporations appear to lack. They grow to a certain point and then, as if

---

[1] De Geus, Arie. *The Living Company: Growth, Learning and Longevity in Business.* Nicholas Brealey Publishing, 1997.

their genes are programmed to self-destruct, they collapse into the sort of lethargy associated with grossly premature old age. Rather than demonstrating mastery of the social process, they operate as talent nodes – vehicles that allow individuals to fulfil an ambition at a certain point in their life's journey before the journey takes them on. Their lack of understanding and proficiency in the management of their social dimensions is ultimately their downfall. Paradoxically, by using they also get used.

The path forward

This book posits two critical things. Firstly, that businesses need to conceive of themselves as social units or, to put it more simply, as societies. Secondly, that if global businesses are to become well-functioning societies, they need to think more like states rather than companies. The benchmark needs to shift.

The roles of nations and companies are currently counterposed. The primary self-appointed role of business is to maximise productive use of its assets, including people, in order to maximise returns to shareholders. The role of government is to create an environment conducive to social stability and to raising the standard of living of its citizens. In the latter, the people are the end. In the former, they are a means. To thrive, large firms need to rewrite the rules – to rebalance the axes. They have to learn to replicate something of the social function of the Nation State. The global company has to create a community that is global and nationless. This, for lack of a better term, we have called the heartland of the corporation.

This implies a shift away from the familiar national focus of most firms. Almost all contemporary corporate strategy is

responsive to national pressures. The imperative to denationalise the corporation, to achieve separation from the state
and genuine global social status, requires a huge shift in
mindset. Most of our thinking is bounded in terms of our
national status. All great economic thinking has been based
on developments within the ambit of the state, from Adam
Smith to John Maynard Keynes – if demand increases so
will supply; if supply increases so will the number of jobs;
if the economy needs stimulation, lower interest rates and
heightened government spending will provide it. That
nation-bound paradigm is still the dominant one. We remain
adamantly intellectually bound in rings of nationalism.
Perhaps the most glaring example of this is the way the
economic might of nations is itself measured. Trade statistics
do not acknowledge goods manufactured in a third country
but sold in another.

Intrinsic to the process of advancement for the nascent
global firm is the requirement that they pull themselves
free of their home states. It is the classic search for self-
identity. Worldwide there are probably no more than a
hundred corporations that could conceive of themselves as
global. It is these firms that drive the bulk of world trade.
That is a staggeringly small number in the context of the
number of large companies that operate nationally in their
home markets, the latter perhaps in excess of fifty thousand.
If the number of meaningful states is now around five
hundred, the world has room enough for at least that number
of corporate states.

In our precursor to this book, *Reinspiring the Corporation*,
we defined the process of achieving social cohesiveness as
'reinspiration'. Reinspiration as a process focused on establishing the community of the firm as the cornerstone of
competitiveness. But its, at the time, unintentional emphasis

was on the essentially national-based business. This book deals with the global business. It focuses on how to take the vibrant corporate community proposed in *Reinspiring the Corporation* and turn it into an enduring global corporate society.

Despite their laggardliness in getting to grips with their social identity, companies do have a window of opportunity created by the uncertainty surrounding the future of the Nation State itself. The Nation State may still reign supreme but its supremacy is not unquestioned. The political process has had to evolve from defending national self-interest in the traditionally xenophobic fashion. It is now recognised by most governments that national protectionism is no longer an option. National players must meet international standards. The national standard is no longer a relevant one. The formation of larger economic units, from NAFTA to the EU, is demanding that nations redefine their economic role.

But, if the Nation State is being challenged by the global forces of economic consolidation, it is also being fractured by the momentum of political subsidiarity. We are now in a period of intense political flux between the pressures of economically motivated regional consolidation and those politically motivated forces of ethnic fragmentation. The influence of regions has accelerated and political power has been significantly devolved. The principle reason for this is the declining ability of national communities to meet the needs of employees and consumers, as social bonds such as family and church have fallen away since 1960. The tensions between the two tectonic plates of integration and fragmentation are mounting.

Returning to where we started out, no-one has successfully answered Roberto Goizueta's quandary – what does

being global mean? What does it demand in terms of the
characteristics of the company? How does that ambition
affect the way geographically dispersed firms should be
managed? Essentially, it all boils down to one question: how
is global competitive advantage achieved? That is the question this book ultimately aims to answer, but with one big
philosophical difference to all its predecessors on the subject.
The emphasis is not on structure or process, it is solely on
people – that strange mélange of blood, guts and soul that
makes the world go round!

2

Corporate schizophrenia: the national Jekyll versus the global Hyde

In the hot Portuguese summer of 1496, Vasco da Gama was poring over a vellum manuscript in the cool stillness of the Santa Maria monastery. Outside, the sun beat down mercilessly on the parched meseta above Lisboa. Priests had been producing maps for hundreds of years – mostly illuminated allegories of the fate of man on earth. The seas were realms of strange fantasy filled with krakens and ship-devouring monsters. The earth was a table of cascading water. The continents were confused masses cobbled together from accounts of traders and mercenaries. Whole sections of what every schoolchild now takes for granted were still blank – places where neither God nor God-fearing man had trodden.

Da Gama had different ideas. He was a man ahead of his time. The abstract continental blobs of his map connoted a world waiting to be painted – islands and peoples to be pencilled in. Even the land mass of continental Europe was imperfectly defined. The East was ambiguous in shape and size. Columbus had even mistaken the Americas for India. This was an age of invention with no bounds other than man's imagination. The act of imagining was one of both intellectual but also very real conquest. The modern Nation State had not been born. Political boundaries were as scant as fences on the plains of the great Midwest of the 1850s. In 1497, five years after his rival Columbus, da Gama embarked on an odyssey to fill in the blanks in man's demonised imagination – an odyssey that would ultimately lead to the creation of an empire.

In the spring of 1839, almost four hundred years later, an impoverished Scottish student, David Livingstone, was bent over an English map of the world in the gloom of his Blantyre tenement. The cloth-backed paper was worn from fingering. As he smoothed it out across his knees, Europe was the centre of the world laid out before him. All the major European countries were portrayed in different garish colours – the pink of Britannia, Prussian blue, the red of the Russian bear, the puce of post-revolutionary France. The pink of Great Britain had spread its insipid stain over half the landmass of the world – India, Ceylon, a scatter of islands in the blue vastness of the Pacific Ocean, assorted archipelagos in the seas of China and Siam, the forested expanse of Canada, and the vast empty continent of Australia. The blue of Prussian Germany, the puce of France, even the yellow of the remnants of the Habsburg Empire – each had spread across the surface of the globe like a series of exotic rashes.

In the almost four hundred years since da Gama, the empty spaces had been reinvented as Empires, under the dominion of the Five Great Powers. The one last uncharted emptiness into which Livingstone's imagination could spill was the dark continent – Africa. He set sail on the *George* in 1840 to fulfil the same act of invention da Gama had centuries before. And, like the inexorable machine of nationhood that da Gama had ignited, the process of understanding was to become quite simply a process of political suzerainty.

In 1987, John Fordham Jr, ensconced in his minimalist office in Washington DC, found himself in a very different position as he stared into the screen of his Mac workstation. The geo orbiting satellite Mardex had been launched a year before. The Earth Orientation Department of the US Naval Observatory which Fordham ran, had leased 10 per cent of its capacity for two years at the heinous cost of $10 million. His mission had exhilarating clarity – to produce a digital map of the earth's surface with enough resolution to isolate an individual football field. It was the sort of objective Fordham's ordered mind excelled at – zero ambiguity. In EOD's digitised rendition of the world, the earth's surface was segmented into those parcels of territory called countries with the precision of a non-linear chessboard.

It had taken almost five hundred years for the blank canvas of the world to be painted out. As we stand here today at the beginning of a new millennium the amount of ambiguity surrounding the portrait of the world is minimal indeed. A few boundaries change in periods of war – as in Bosnia or the Congo. A few agglomerations vanish, as with the demise of the red smear of the Soviet Union. Political adherences shift. But, underlying it all, our world is irrevocably divided into Nation States and, below them, regional states. Each has a name and a capital city. Every significant political dispute usually involves a further fragmentation of larger political units into even more microscopically delineated packages of territory. The level of specificity is increasing, not decreasing.

There are no blank spaces left for the twenty-first century Livingstone or da Gama to fill. Even Hitler's horrific expansionism in the 1930s failed permanently to redefine this distribution. Our physical presence on this earth is defined and prescribed by the Nation State. We are simply born with a national allegiance and wander through the rest with a passport and obligatory return ticket.

The corollary of this fact is that the world is defined by the currency of the Nation State. That currency is called politics. Politics conditions the interaction between the building blocks of society. Whether a river is dammed, a rail link endorsed, a building zone changed, a war started or a resolution enforced – all are political decisions. In a world segmented into Nation States, it is politics and not economics that drives behaviour.

The primacy of the political unit of the Nation State is not an easy fact to accommodate for a man like Niall Fitzgerald sitting at his desk overlooking the Thames from Unilever House at Blackfriars. On the one hand, a firm like Unilever has to serve nationally distinct tastes. But on the other, unless it can achieve global scale in its core brands, its profitability will continually disappoint. The only point of being big is to exploit scale economies, to exercise muscle. The world map of the corporation is inevitably torn between an imperative for globalism and the constraints imposed by the primacy of the Nation State.

As he sits at his London desk, he also has to reflect that the issue of national markets is not simply about consumer tastes. More profoundly it is also a matter of the identity of the firm itself. Most big companies are highly nationally focused and derive their strength from national origins, whether Sony in Japan or Coca-Cola in the US. This fact imposes critical limitations which cannot be ignored.

Fitzgerald has to accept that the Anglo-Dutch identity of his own firm may impose its own restrictions on the evolution of the firm beyond Blackfriars.

Tearing up the maps – the fundamental imperative to go global

This is not a state of affairs most corporations have been content to accept. Nor would it appear they have done so. Over the past ten years one thing would appear to have changed the business environment more than any other single factor – globalisation. All significant companies would appear to have a life that transcends their national home market. Peer groups are international guerrillas, not national stars. Competitiveness is no longer discussed as a national concept, despite the fact that every metric is measured nationally – from market share, to growth, to GDP per capita. The lifeblood of business – capital – now operates fluidly across borders. The corporate titans have torn up the maps refined by politicians and their cartographers over the preceding thousand years.

This sea change has brought with it extraordinary pressures to bear on large firms, and particularly non-US firms who lack the gargantuan home market. US companies were drawn into globalisation far earlier than other national enterprises in the wake of the pervasive US military presence following the Second World War. The impetus was political, not economic. But, most importantly, it has not meant any real change for US corporations. The home market still dominates the sales line of most. The de facto adoption of the dollar as the global unit of trade, combined with the ubiquitous dissemination of US-style management education and management consultancy, has allowed US firms to achieve international viability without substantively altering their nationally based practices. It is quite literally cultural imperialism and it has brought enormous economic benefit to all.

This pattern does not hold true for non-US corporates. Whilst most non-US firms derive their culture and management from their home market, many still have to make a concerted effort to break those roots. The reason is simple: the home market is diminutive compared to the international opportunity. Perhaps the industry where the transition has been most dramatic is that of the increasingly deregulated telcos. British Telecom has rebranded itself as the androgynous BT, Finnish Telecom as Senora, and Deutsche Telekom as the elusive Telekom. Similarly, the national airlines are increasingly striving to evolve from being flag carriers to participating in global networks through alliances, whether One World or Star Alliance. In 1996 British Airways even went so far as to shed its flag altogether. But national ties are not so easily broken. Every country pretty much still reserves the right to approve or disapprove the sale of its airlines. The US even has a law prohibiting foreign ownership over 20 per cent! It should not therefore be too surprising that BA is reinstating the Union Jack in the face of disaffection amongst its business traveller loyalists.

Whatever the individual circumstances, most firms seem to perceive that remaining wedded to a national definition of competitiveness is a doomed strategy, the same as xenophobia has always proved to be the poorest form of pursuing self-interest. This puts them under huge strains, particularly as they increasingly bang headlong into issues of national interest. The globalisation of firms is misconstrued by many politicians to be a real threat to the interest of the Nation State. The catalyst, of course, is fear of the loss of manufacturing jobs – the superstition that fickle MNCs are solely in the game of finding the lowest cost labour and that it is this rapacious motive which drives globalisation. The most graphic evocation of this spectre was Ross Perot's infamous sucking sound as jobs headed Mexico-way in the wake of NAFTA. The same storm has been whipped up by BMW's break-up of the benighted Rover in the UK. The reality, however, is that it is the relentless fulfilment of the urge towards growth, not the pursuit of low wages, that is driving globalisation. Far from being a threat to the Nation State, the issue for the firm is how viably to break free of a national grip that is almost irresistible.

Riding the vortex of consolidation

Such an impetus to globalise could not be satisfied by organic growth alone. Organic growth takes decades, not months. Hunger for rapid global scale can only be satiated through acquisition. It should not, therefore, be surprising that the urge to denationalise has resulted in a blizzard of M&A activity. Over the past ten years, all sectors from advertising through to pharmaceuticals have experienced unprecedented rates of consolidation. And the pace is not relenting. All industries have gone through cyclical phases of fragmentation, as a result of technological specialisation, followed by agglomeration. This has tracked the maturation of every field of human endeavour from farming through to manufacture of computer chips. But now the scale and momentum is of a different order.

In 1999 the annual value of mergers and acquisitions broke the trillion dollar mark for the first time in history. And the M&A figures do not even include the value of alliances that do not involve equity. By 1995 the average rate of alliance formation was greater than ten thousand companies world-wide, a tenfold increase from 1990. Corning, the US glass manufacturer, for example, reported 1998 sales of $6 billion, but if the value of alliances was included that number would have leaped to $12 billion! These alliances often tend grad-ually to assume an equity nature as relationships mature. The car industry is a classic example of creeping equity consolidation. It is probable that at least two mega-giants will eventually emerge, each involving Ford/GM, Toyota/Honda/Nissan or two from amongst the ten or so current competitors in Europe.

Consolidation within national boundaries – even large ones such as the United States – have their natural limits before competition is eradicated. And should a firm achieve an imminently monopolistic position, most countries have anti-competition acts and their equivalent of Glass Steagall to remedy the situation in consumers' interests. The regula-tory war with Microsoft has even been waged at the risk of destabilising the Nasdaq. Consolidation therefore has its regulatory limits within the context of the Nation State and business is subjugated to the will of the national community expressed through the political framework.

But contemporary consolidation is a very different beast. It knows no national boundaries. If national regulation in a home market limits the opportunity to merge and acquire, then there is always the international market. Cross-border M&A deals surpassed domestic ones for the first time in 1996, with a total value of $600 billion. There is no effective regu-latory body to manage market share on a regional or global basis, other than the EU competition authority in Brussels. Market share is almost invariably measured by national market.

Most of the new, so-called global companies have become global through rapid deal doing. Consolidating across borders poses a fundamentally new challenge for intrinsically nation-centric firms. Once the deal is done and the bankers paid off, the acquirer has to manage the acquired. National firms acquired by an international aggressor tend to cling to their national traditions with a vengeance. The nexus of the Nation State exerts its inexorable pull. The analogy with military expansionism is an apt one. Many empires – from Charlemagne to the Ottomans – have expanded aggressively overseas through the military equivalent of hostile acquisitions. But their longevity is invariably finite compared to that of the political entities they temporarily draw into their fold. The ethnic fissures of distinct cultures remain. The same is true of most corporations. The firm globalising through acquisition is often fighting the ethnic and cultural grain.

The painfulness of this process and frailty of the veneer over many of these so-called global corporate structures is fundamentally misunderstood by the capital markets that place a value on them. The capital markets themselves are globalising with ease because they treat the world homogeneously. Their customers and constituents all value cash equally and evaluate risks on a fairly standardised basis. The investment banks that create the market are also homogeneous in culture, dominated by Wall Street and with a mutual churn of personnel between them that ensures practices are shared almost instantaneously. A Frankfurt-based banker is not so distinct from his Wall Street brethren, particularly as they will now often work for the same group.

Most companies are simply not like that. They are not populated by global, MBA-speaking citizens. The result is a sort of suppressed schizophrenia between a management espousing a global strategy and an employee base wedded to local identity, many of whom will have been 'acquired' along with their firm. The more deals are done, the more the society of the enlarged firm fragments into cultural silos. When the tides of strategic sentiment turn, the veneer of one-firmness quickly falls away. There is no social fraternity in deal doing! The ease with which BMW could emotionally extract itself from Rover, a business which it acquired amid great fanfares only five years before, is a glaring example.

The global myth versus multinational reality

It is for this reason that, whatever the high-falutin management literature may claim, the dominant model of management for an international firm is the multinational model. The multinational was invented in the 1950s in the wake of US corporate expansion after the war. It typically connotes exactly what it says – a confederation of local national operations connected by common ownership at a minimum and hopefully something more. But usually not much more!

Most so-called global businesses are in fact multi-local businesses – a matrix of local operations run by local people and overseen by a remote group of corporate functionaries responsible for control, treasury and M&A. In almost all cases, the seminal decisions are set by the home market, whether in New York or Tokyo, from strategy through to R&D, product design, brand essence and capital commitments. There is clearly a difference between those firms that grow organically overseas and those that acquire. But the rate of globalisation makes the former route strategically inevitable. With it comes multinationalism as surely as night follows day. Both management and analysts are aware of this of course. In their resulting anxiety to wrest control over the strategy of the acquired, acquirers usually wind up eroding value. That is why only 20 per cent of deals deliver share-holder payback. It all comes down to race and ethnicity.

A world of stumbling home-boy giants

The world's largest 500 companies account for 80 per cent of foreign direct investment and half of world trade. Of these, 440 come from rich home countries and dominantly the US and Japan. The number of global firms is small – far smaller than the number of significant countries in which they operate. Logic would suggest that their power should be mounting, even if not to the heights attained by the East India Company in the 1800s.

But the truth of the matter is that very few firms, if any, are truly global. For a firm to be global it cannot by defini-tion be national. It cannot rely on national characteristics to define its community. It has to define its own society, detached from its founding national roots. It is not global in any real sense if it is tethered to its home state because of the allegiance of its key people. The average large firm is no more than forty years old at best. By contrast, the average modern Nation State has been extant in more or less its current form since 1870. In this tussle between national and global identity, multinational businesses risk the perils of social schizophrenia. As with its human counterpart, schizo-phrenia is not a viable condition for a healthy life.

One key underlying reason for their ephemerality appears to be that the average corporation has not yet found its own global identity, as distinct from its identification with its home Nation State. In the human analogy, it has not left home and grown up! This amounts to saying that the average corporation has not created its own society which can rival that of its home state in terms of commanding the allegiance of its people. If firms are to achieve longevity and power they need to develop their societies independent of the state. This is as much as saying they need to become corporate states in their own right.

The core characteristic of successful societies is that they have cohesive communities at their heart and, often, many of them. These communities are bound together by a shared concept of citizenship, founded on a plethora of shared and embedded customs, laws and mores. In our precursive book, *Reinspiring the Corporation*, we explored how firms could develop such cohesive communities. This was principally conceived of on a national basis where many of the social ingredients of such a community concept were already in place. Achieving social cohesion on a global basis is a very different proposition! It is that which we will explore in later chapters.

But firstly, if we are proposing the formation of corporate states, we must understand the foundations of the Nation State which is the best role model we have of how to form and manage a society. Clever people have spent at least three hundred years ideating the role and shape of the Nation State. The formal science of business strategy by comparison is only thirty years old at most. Therefore, we as strategists have plenty to learn from wiser minds!

3

Creating societies:
the case of the Nation State

Despite the global dreams, we have to accept that states are the essential units of world society. People are represented in the UN through their states. Commodity trade is between nations, as are of course most wars! The Nation State defines who we are. If posed the seminal question, 'what are you?', most people would respond 'American, British or Basque' and not 'an IBM or Motorola executive'.

In most countries there is a social contract between citizen and state. The specific nature of the contract varies and is shaped by the culture of the people it unites. Most of Western society finds its philosophical and social roots in Rousseau and Jefferson, founded on the Enlightenment precept of 'reason'. In this contract between managers and managed, managers are both subjects and rulers. The contract empowers elected government to act on behalf of its citizens and, in order to fulfil that obligation, the state retains the right to levy taxes and enforce laws. To work, the contract has to be endorsed by at least the majority of those it binds together. This usually means that participants in the contract share fundamental beliefs, shaped by common culture and, in most instances outside the US, by common ethnic roots.

The governmental process of the modern Nation State has three critical characteristics that frame the social contract:

- It is founded on democratic representation.
- Its principal role is serving the collective interests of its population and its population is prepared to pay for this service through taxes and more extreme pledges in times of collective need, such as war.
- It understands that, in order to meet its obligations, it has a central role to play in managing the economy, much as a board of governors oversees the management of a social institution, but without direct control of factors of production, except in times of national emergency.

These may sounds like platitudes, but before 1900 the state had a very different conception of its purpose. By contrast, it was characterised by:

- Dominance of a hereditary political elite.
- A principal self-appointed role in furthering the interests of government.
- A laissez-faire view of distributive economic responsibility, combined with defence of the vested commercial privileges and interests of elite stakeholders.

In essence, the old Nation State before the First World War was much more akin to the modern corporation, than to the modern Nation State. Like the modern corporation, its locus of attention was on the interests of the powerful elite of stake-holders – analogous to institutional investors. It had little concept of the need to be responsive to its citizens. Nor did it perceive that its best route to longevity was to focus on bettering the lot of its citizens. Although conceived three thousand years ago in Homer's Greece, the concept of citizenship as the foundation of a reciprocal social contract has only really been extant for the last hundred years. In the corporate world, there is as yet no substantive evidence that the concept is taken seriously at all. To understand the relevance of its application to the corporation, we must understand in more detail the evolution of the Nation State from its old to modern forms.

Life before the Nation State

Nationalism has old roots. As far back as 1648, the multi-nation treaties of Westphalia had formally recognised the existence of separate sovereignties in one society of nations and had stipulated that states were equal as well as inter-dependent. But the reality is that modern national democracies date essentially from 1900. It is a relatively young form of social organisation.

Before the Nation State was the prince and, following in his typically bloody trail, the elite government of nobles. The innumerable rivalries of the sixteenth and seventeenth centuries were rivalries between dynastic rulers. It was a time of skirmishes and fortified towns when travel between communities was a hazardous undertaking. The eighteenth century was marked by the abandonment of dynastic princi-ples in favour of considerations of *raison d'état*, whereby state authority was vested in a typically hereditary leader. This principle of leadership took a hundred years to evolve from Louis XIV's 'L'état c'est moi', to Frederick the Great of Prussia's avowed pride in being the first servant of the people or state. But even as late as 1750 it was the afterglow of the medieval concept of divine right that still legitimised the role of monarchy in the popular mind. It was an external, inscrutable authority.

The birth of the modern Nation State was a revolution against such external authority. Kant and the philosophers of the Enlightenment proposed rule by reason rather than subservience to a preordained order. When these ideas were translated into practice, they gave rise to the representative state as people rose up against their rulers and captured the power of the sovereign. It was this rule of reason, based on the growing supremacy of science, that became embedded in the Declaration of Independence. Kant envisaged a world heading towards a perpetual peace whose twin pillars were Republican government and international organisation, cemented by the steady expansion of the rule of law. George Hegel, like Kant before him, conceived of mankind as progressing through various stages of organisation to a culminating point of a rational state of being.

Although by 1800 the concept of the state had institutionalised what had been a personalised, hereditary system of rule, it did not really alter the way governments interacted with each other. The main preoccupation of the state government was ensuring its own continued existence against the threat of foreign powers. The idea that the state should be preoccupied about securing its support by the population at large, or indeed even securing their economic prosperity, was still nowhere to be seen in practice. This view was also implicitly endorsed by the political philosophers of the day.

Kant, like Rousseau before him, held the view that international conflict made progress possible. All ends were political.

It was not until the 1830s that economics began to assume due importance alongside political ambitions. This sea change was largely prompted by the rise of the US and UK during the Industrial Revolution. The preoccupation with political and military competition between governments was replaced by an imperative to secure a well-functioning and wealthy society. International political rivalries were increasingly held in check by a system of international law. It was Bentham and Mill who promoted the idea that peace would be achieved by replacing relations between states with relations between societies and their nations.

By the 1850s the increasing complexity of industrialised life had forced governments to become more representative and just regulators of their communities. They began to ally with the dynamic force of national principle as a means of advancing their interests. The result was greater national cohesion and the emergence of national sentiment concentrated on the symbols of the state – from flags through to national anthems and teacups depicting the Queen, or fans embroidered with the First Lady. The socialism of the 1870s was a natural successor to the liberalism of the 1850s. The participatory contract with the citizen that was to blossom fully in the 1930s began to take its shape.

It was not until 1900 that the modern state began to emerge. In tandem with the growth in scientific knowledge, the development of the modern state gathered real momentum after 1914 with the outbreak of the First World War. The emphasis of political power shifted decisively from manpower and size of territory to industrial and scientific ability. But it was only after the slaughter at the Somme and

Passchendaele that public opinion emerged decisively as a serious check on government action. Before 1914 it is almost impossible to find evidence that French, British or US public opinion ever acted as a deterrent in foreign policy. It is equally impossible to show that French, British or US foreign policy has not been conditioned by public opinion since 1914–18. The notion had at last gathered momentum that government exists for man, not man for government – almost three hundred years after Westphalia.

It had taken three hundred years to progress from a situation where the state was no longer the instrument of the competitive ambitions of governmental elites. It now had broadly to reflect the interests of its constituencies. This evolution of purpose was to a significant extent a function of fast-evolving and increasingly dispersed scientific knowledge. Democratisation has always gone hand in hand with scientific advancement and diffusion of the tools of knowledge and production. As we shall come on to, the explosion of the Internet will almost certainly have the same acceleratory impact on autocratic states worldwide.

The rise of the Nation State as CEO

Prior to 1914, governments had not assumed explicit responsibility for running the economies that financed them. The twentieth century, by contrast, witnessed an unprecedented expansion of state economic intervention. The Great War demonstrated what the state could accomplish through mobilisation when it needed to increase production to meet its political objectives. During the heavy unemployment of the 1920s, the pressure was on the state to find a solution and it returned to its wartime experience. Once again, following the end of the Second World War, the Bretton Woods accords made governments directly responsible for managing their national economies in order to meet citizens' growing demands for a higher standard of living and employment. The feat of national economic expansion from the ashes of the apocalypse was a government charter. The UN charter itself enshrined governments' responsibility to cooperate in order to regulate and guarantee a viable world market for trade.

This dirigist imperative had initially been leavened in the 1930s by the influence of John Maynard Keynes whose thesis was to make the market rather than the bureaucracy the instrument for indirect planning. The role of government was to encourage investment through tax planning and similar measures, and to stimulate consumption. But by the 1950s, with the petering out of the reconstruction boom and under the threat of Khrushchev's export deluge, governments again lost their nerve and seized the tiller in an effort to sustain growth. Government spending shot from 20 per cent of GDP in 1960 to 43 per cent in 1980 and had reached 45 per cent by 1990, augmented by public subsidies. Even the crusade launched by Thatcher and Reagan in the early 1980s to roll back the state only succeeded in nudging this back to 41 per cent. The state's neo-Keynesian hand in directing economic activity remains paramount, driven by its increased responsibility for protecting the interests of its citizens.

The rise of the democratic principle

But it was not until the 1970s that this new-found social contract decisively took on its modern form in all Western states. In the mid-1970s first Greece and then Portugal threw aside their totalitarian regimes in favour of democratically elected governments. Then, in 1978, Franco's death at last allowed the ossified Spain to thaw. This set off a wave that, by the mid-1990s, had washed over much of Latin America and Central Europe and even lapped at the doors of states as far flung as Korea and Taiwan. As we stand here in 2001 the crest of that great surge has even begun to permeate the great Chinese wall of Maoism. In 1975, 68 per cent of the 140 states in the world were dictatorships. By 1995 this had shrunk to 28 per cent out of an enlarged total of 190 states. As with all change, it tends to accelerate exponentially.

This has been accompanied by an emphatic shift from state-led growth to market-oriented policies. Not surprisingly, therefore, the ascendancy of liberal democracy has been accompanied by an explosion of privatisation – the liberation of enterprise from direct political intervention. The capitalised value of privatisation was $13 billion in 1990, mostly concentrated in utilities such as infrastructure and telcos. By 1996, this had risen to $156 billion and had spread out from traditional government-controlled sectors to financial services and manufacturing.

It is tempting to assert that there exists a natural correlation between the rise of economic market values and democracy. But things are not so simple. Some of the fastest adopters of the Western market model in the early 1990s were dictatorships rather than liberal democracies – from Taiwan to Malaysia. And the pattern of democracy has varied dramatically between economic dirigism and laissez-faire. What is clear, however, is that the Nation State has evolved from being elitist and managerial-centric to being representative and inclusive, the government vested with broad economic responsibility but without equity control of the factors of production. As we shall get on to, this has its precise analogy in the corporate world.

The foundations of the society of the state

The social contract between people and state has evolved over three hundred years. It has suffered its stresses and strains, and, as we will explore presently, it continues to do so. But as we stand here today, it is the most enduring institution in all our lives, defines who we are and prescribes our relationship with our fellow man. In an era of intense individualism and pervasive isolation, it is what satisfies our social instincts.

The basis of the modern social contract between state and people is founded on the concept of citizenship. Citizenship is a reciprocal contract that grants the state the right to demand fulfilment of personal obligations in order that it should satisfy the collective needs of the majority of its constituents. The healthiness of this reciprocal arrangement determines the cohesiveness of a nation's people into a single society. The weaker and more ineffectual it is, the more the nation fragments into multiple and often competing societies. The single, unified society, where citizens' relationships with that society are broadly aligned, is a powerful one. It is also compelling enough to overcome ethnic divisions – the scourge of the Nation State.

Part of the basis of that contract relates of course to the relatively primitive issue of collective security – that together we can better defend our interests than we could alone. At this level, society is simply an adult extension of the playground gang. In our post-millennium society, with the threat of nuclear stand-off now fading, the focus of social security is economic. The basis of the contemporary social contract is that the society of the state will ensure with reasonable certainty a minimum degree of economic security. It does so through managing fiscal and monetary policy, sustaining an appropriate regulatory environment and through equitable redistribution of wealth via taxation.

The core basis of the citizen–state contract is, of course, that set of social rules called the law. The law is an explicit code governing our relationships with each other and with the state itself. The legal system tends to be unique to each Nation State – a sort of indigenous social DNA. But at heart the legal process is about ensuring that we behave in a way that is compatible with the general good. We could, after all, probably benefit most decisively in the short term by pursuing entirely selfish goals – whether driving down bus lanes or forging signatures on cheques. But the collective effect of this would, of course, be ultimately self-defeating, even if we didn't perceive it that way now. At its most abstract level, the state law is there to make us condition our behaviour to achieve collective outcomes rather than maximise individual outcomes. Perhaps the most tangible aspect of that surrender of individualism is the payment of taxes. By paying tax we buy civilisation. The fact that most entrepreneurs and large businesses invest huge efforts in tax minimisation is symptomatic of the prevailing obliviousness to the role of social glue in making organisations competitive. And social glue does not come free of charge!

Does that mean that it is only a legal framework that checks a deterioration into mayhem? That the society of the Nation State is built solely on rules? Clearly, this is not so. Any institution founded solely on rules will ultimately fail for the simple reason that human nature dictates that such limitations on intellectual movement have to be surmounted. The rule of force inspires rebellion. The intellectual prescription of what we should and should not think stokes the all-consuming fires of subversion. One is reminded of the analogy of a tree ultimately engulfing railings. It is in the nature of organic things to break their bounds.

All social systems ultimately have to balance rules with positive motivators. Rules provide checks. Motivators instigate forward motion, if applied within a broad, constructive design. In the case of national society, one of these positive motivators is morality – the system of values that defines what makes us feel good about what we do. All sound and well-functioning Nation States have at their core a set of values that every member of that society at least acknowledges, even if they do not espouse them. Living out these values and gaining acknowledgment as an exemplar of such virtues is a form of personal salvation. Morality ultimately defines our progress through life. Cash cannot play that role alone.

The decline of the institution of the church has, of course, taken its toll on formal morality – the sort of morality that is codified and explicit. But that does not mean morality has gone away. All nations are distinguished by overlapping but unique concepts of what is and is not acceptable. In France topless bathing and mistresses are not cardinal sins. In Ireland they are! A moral code is a vital part of feeling good about what we do. More profoundly, it is responsible for giving us a constructive set of aspirations. Morality in this broader sense blurs at the edges with concepts of peer admiration and social endorsement. Otherwise, as in drug states such as Colombia and Panama, we would all simply rob our way to greatness. There is an ambition in most respectable people that craves the sort of acknowledgement only indirectly furnished by a wad of greenbacks.

Beyond contractual to emotional
terms of engagement

Clearly, the provision of economic security and a legal frame-work is not where the social contract between state and individual ends. Otherwise everyone would emigrate to Swit-zerland or Sweden! There is clearly a set of more abstract, but also more profound, factors that condition people's rela-tionship with the society that is the Nation State. Too often this intangible set of factors is crudely bundled into that anachronistic notion 'patriotism'. Calling participation in national society 'patriotism' is like labelling all psychological problems as insanity. It was perhaps an adequate gloss a hun-dred years ago. But now such simplification is unacceptable.

It is one of the extraordinary characteristics of the Nation State that we as individuals are prepared to be held in check by an economic/legal system which ostensibly would appear to cramp our individual style. Clearly, the only reason we submit ourselves willingly to a collective will is that we have faith we will do better together than alone. Not everyone shares this faith. Guernsey, Jersey, the BVIs, Bermuda and a scatter of other far-flung islands are populated by exiles who would prefer to keep their tax money and forgo the pleasures of participating in a national framework. But this is an infin-itesimally small minority. It is a fundamental tenet of the society of the state that we as citizens opt for a mutually supportive context that values collective outcomes, rather than hole up alone in a tax haven. It is this implicit abne-gation of individualism that marks out successful societies. We are individuals for sure, but with an appreciation that we ultimately share the fate of our neighbours.

Among the emotive forces binding together the societies of states, the most glaringly obvious are all the manifestations of national identity. All countries share a common reverence for the symbols of statehood – they mark out their own society as being distinct from any other. In its most traditional form, this manifests itself in flags and anthems. But in its more subtle form it reflects itself in clothing, music and other outward expression, or what might rather belittlingly be labelled under the sobriquet 'taste'. The French like snails, the Americans pretzels. The Germans like order, the Spanish conviviality. The Italians make love, the English polite conversation. The physical expressions of nationality may not be as explicit as tribal tattoos but they are ingrained and profound. Most states are no longer ethnically homogeneous, but they do typically share a common language, an accent, mannerisms, taboos and joys. An Englishman abroad will immediately identify another and also invariably identify with them.

Shared identity is powerful because it typically has continuity. No potent social identity can be invented overnight. That is what makes the continual makeovers that characterise the modern corporation such a shallow sleight-of-hand. They may trick the external world into believing that there is something new but they typically fail to convince insiders. The distinct social identities of Nation States have been forged over centuries. That historical continuity is central to their enduring potency. We all like to think that we have a past to be proud of. It is part of a positive sense of self-worth. In the case of national societies, that continuity is manifested in a plethora of enduring characteristics – from the orchestrated pageants, to celebrations of history, through to more embedded traits such as 'old wives' tales' and turns of phrase. At every turn there are continual reminders of our social past and the appreciation of that past binds us together as a society. The principle of pastness even extends to the law. In the

Anglo-Saxon legal system at least, society is governed by principles based explicitly on past precedent.

Of all the aspects of our sense of pastness, one is probably more potent than any other – our thirst for mystery. Mystery is intimately bound up with positivism. If something is not fully comprehensible it invites conjecture; it holds the hope of something great. Mystery is bound up with the possibility of redemption. It inspires awe. When our lives are transparent and routine, we invent it, from ET through to ESP. The Nation State is shrouded in such mystery. The British have their pugnacious origins in Boudicca, in the round table of King Arthur, on the fields of Crécy and Agincourt. America finds its apotheosis in the shadowy figures of Custer and Grant, in the mystical encounter between the Pilgrim Fathers and the native Indian who speaks perfect King James English on the desolate emptiness of Plymouth Rock. The formation of the society of the state is a semi-mystical event – as with the birth of any great social institution, through from Christianity to Buddhism.

In most contexts, the obsession with pastness would be attributed to entrenchment, to lack of progress. But the relationship between citizen and state is far from anti-progressive. Despite its continuity the social contract between state and citizen is not a static one. Most institutions falter precisely because of their rigidity. Great institutions are usually founded through intellectual revolution. But they typically end where they began – held in a deadlock by a hierarchy defending vested interests they will not yield up. It is the old man's syndrome – he who defends himself from impending death by clinging on to power. The democratic process of the modern democracy has as its premise the rejection of such ossification. At the heart of it is the principle of accountability, enshrined in the medium of the vote. The vote guarantees debate and usually heated debate. If there is one thing that characterises successful Nation States it is precisely such an ingrained process of self-questioning. As soon as the questioning stops, when the democratic debate is silenced, then the rot sets in and the whole system deteriorates.

A corollary of the process of debate and representation is the faith that improvement is possible. Policy making is a dynamic of perpetual refinement and adaptation, of reconciling distinct viewpoints that are continually counter-posed. If one side cannot deliver, it will swiftly be out and the other side will get a crack of the whip. The possibility of change and improvement through exercising the collective voice makes the society of the Nation State a fundamentally optimistic one. If people believe in something and shout loudly enough legislation will surely follow. Even if changes take years to institute, the existence of the possibility of influencing collective outcomes means that fatalism and pacifism are undermined. With that also disappears the risk of dictatorship.

Towards a set of universal principles

The society of the state hardly appears to be a society at all. It is characterised by vociferous babble, and comprised of competing political parties whipped up by fractious debates. Consensus is actively forced through vocal confrontation. The system is periodically violently purged. All would seem chaotic and ill disciplined. But held within a framework of continuity of identity and heritage, it provides an enduring force for social cohesion. No developed democratic state has yet suffered a civil war. No developed

Figure 3.1   The fundamental characteristics of the society of the
Nation State

democratic state has collapsed from within. By contrast, virtually no company has escaped either fate.

   But, equally, none is without a comparatively uniform set
of foundation stones. Beyond the basic objectives of achieving economic security and preserving a viable legal system of
rules, the society of the Nation State would appear to be
founded on seven core heartland characteristics:

1   A moral framework of social governance.
2   A fiscal and legal context focused on collective outcomes.
3   A common idiom and identity.
4   A shared sense of heritage founded on a rich social
    history.
5   An institutionalised process of remorseless self-question-
    ing and examination.

6 An ingrained and optimistic pursuit of human betterment.

7 A cultivated sense of cultural mystery.

These are not perhaps the qualities that would normally be
classified as drivers of nationhood. As with companies, in
assessing the strength of countries we so often focus on
outputs such as GNP per capita and factor productivity. But,
interestingly, these do appear to be qualities shared by the
other great social institutions in our lives. In our precursor
to this book, *Reinspiring the Corporation*, we explored that
other great set of social institutions – the great religious
movements – to determine what characteristics made them
such potent and enduring social forces and whether they held
any important lessons for corporations. Perhaps not surprisingly, there is a large degree of overlap between the core
societal characteristics of the Nation State and of the great
religions. Not surprisingly because they are the only large-
scale institutions that have retained any stability as a medium
for harnessing man's productive energies and restraining his
destructive impulses.

The world's seven great religious movements – Christianity, Judaism, Hinduism, Confucianism, Taoism, Buddhism and
Islam – all seem to share the same fundamental characteristics. Whilst immensely diverse in their practices and in the
philosophical foundation of their observances, if all their
particular qualities are stripped back, the great religious
movements share seven common qualities through which
they appear to inspire adherence in people:

1 They provide a context of moral authority and a framework which offers the chance for personal spiritual
redemption.

2   They emphasise looking beyond the individual and the primacy of integration or surrender to collective interests for a good which is beyond limited self-interest.
3   They are characterised by deeply ingrained ritual and symbolism.
4   Their progress is founded on well-understood tradition.
5   They encourage the asking of the big questions.
6   They are essentially optimistic in their outlook; their view of the competitive universe is positive.
7   They cloak themselves in mystery; they are not easily understood.

These seven characteristics are pervasive in all seven great religious movements. They also appear to be fundamental to the character of the democratic Nation State. So there is every reason to believe they are there to satisfy a profound psycho-sociological need in all of us – to respond to a set of core needs we all share and which we spend most of our lives consciously or unconsciously trying to satisfy. It is these needs which unite us all in our humanity, namely:

1. The universal need we all share to perceive an order that puts definition on our individual efforts, which shows that we can contribute something that has meaning, that confirms that what we are doing is good and that there will be a reward for the trials and tribulations it involves. This is the salve to the incipient threat of futility we all face at one time or another.

The context of moral authority is the necessary framework which provides some guarantee that the positive efforts we have put in will lead somewhere. That they will bring endorsement, recognition. That we should not simply stay in bed or ransack the shopping mall. That behaving properly is a better approach. That we should continue to strive.

In the case of the great religions, this authority is not only worldly, it is divine. It infuses our consciousness with a line of delineation – between the things we should feel good about and the things we should feel ashamed of. Although we commonly refer back to the Ten Commandments of Christianity, the Eightfold Path of Buddhism or the Seven Pillars of Islam, the moral imperative is more than simply a set of dictates. The context of moral authority tends to be so ingrained in one form or another in most of us that we don't perceive it as a stipulation at all. We perceive it as a personal quality. That is testimony to its success in fashioning our motivations.

In the case of the Nation State, the context of moral authority is enshrined in law. But none of us are governed solely by consideration of the law or we would continually be hauled up in front of magistrates' courts. We all also tend to obey a non-codified common law which conditions our behaviour and defines our national character. The average American has a keen sense of their right to free speech and of the defence of their liberties, even using the trusty Smith & Wesson if necessary. The First and Second Amendments are ingrained in national behaviour. Americans also find it morally laudable to engage energetically in free enterprise. Wealth carries no stigma. The British, by contrast, appear to value fairness and doing the right thing. Until recently, the pursuit of unbridled wealth had negative social connotations. For Southern Europeans morality is bound up with family and lineage. Honour and defence of family honour assumes almost messianic proportions. Morality is an affair of the blood.

Aspiring to the dominant morality of our society is what fuels our aspirations – aspirations largely for recognition. The goal may appear egocentric and individualistic, but it is in fact intensely social – to conform with and excel at what our fellow man values. That is why many extremely wealthy people tend towards philanthropy. There is no higher goal than social recognition. It is also why peerages and knighthoods still obsess the fifty-something British CEO. Morality provides us with a yardstick of personal progress which is enshrined in the fabric of the Nation State. Belonging is everything.

2. The universal need we all have to escape from the locked cell of our ego. We are all inclined to view the world from our own perspective of personal preoccupation. If an event occurs, from a collapse in the stock market to a hurricane in the West Indies, we will all tend to absorb the event from the personal perspective of whether it will disrupt our retirement or jeopardise our holiday plans. We might feel some remorse for the people victimised, but usually with reference to quiet personal relief that we are not involved, or that our portfolio has remained intact.

Self-interest is, as we all now know, a natural corollary of biological selection. Darwin spotted that one almost two hundred years ago – the selfish gene. But it is also profoundly limiting and unsettling. Unique self-focus means that individual setbacks assume vast proportions. That we can derive no real joy from collective success. That our relationships with others are always tainted with competitiveness; 'Sure, I'm glad for him, but just perhaps I'd like to see him fall flat on his face . . .'.

The product of competitiveness is isolation – her versus me. The next twenty years promise to be characterised by extreme individual competitiveness. The emphasis on socialised competitiveness has never been greater. They also promise to be the most lonely and, quite literally, divorced years for many of us. Separation appears not to be a natural condition. We are all at heart social creatures. As well as admiration, we all crave companionship. That is why extreme competition produces psychological dysfunctionality.

The question is what possible point of connection can we forge in our competitive world where we are ranked one against another? Are we doomed to competitive isolation? The great religions say no. Community, shared beliefs, alignment with collective interest are the dominant psychological needs; more dominant than the drive for individual accomplishment. This would suggest we have our role models all wrong. The obsessive focus on individualism, on competitiveness, is actually a mistake. We all long for a higher collective purpose; a reunification. This in fact leads to greater satisfaction and therefore invites greater effort from us.

The society of the Nation State is a product of precisely that impulse. It is founded on (at least partial) surrender of personal interests to the rule of collective interests. It has its misty roots in the need for group protection from predators but has obviously evolved a long way since the demise of the sabre-toothed tiger. From the payment of taxes to the use of public transport, we all have to abnegate the impulse to individual selfishness in the knowledge that we do not occupy the land alone. The social contract between citizen and state has at its core the precept of sociability. We all have an individual vote, but it only means anything when the majority of us exercise our right to vote together. Despite our proclaimed thirst for individuality, we all participate in formative social events – from jury service, to voting, to blood donation, to state pension schemes. Our degree of preparedness to do these things relates directly to the competitiveness of the Nation State as a social institution. Most people would be appalled to see their national flag burned before their eyes. Ten million died on the sword of that sentiment through two world wars.

The impulse to participation in a society is so strong that it conditions the peculiar behavioural routines we develop to remain within the magic circle. And there is nothing that most people fear more than exclusion from the magic circle. We all find aberrant behaviour hard to deal with. The hallmarks of non-participation – begging, drunkenness, dilapidation, insanity – scare us. The British even feel uncomfortable showing affection in public! Rejection from the group is a soul-destroying event for most. That is why exile has classically been the ultimate punishment before death. Even the expatriate communities that dot the globe – from Zambia to Fiji – tend to parrot with almost absurd fanaticism the national eccentricities of their home state. Most of us are driven by the urge to seek inclusion, not individualism.

3. The need we all share for the security of ritual. Our lives are fundamentally ritualised; through from the daily routine of waking and preparing for work, to the habit of slumping at night in a favourite chair. The act of repetition reassures us that life is predictable, controllable; that what we do has an order that is both enduring and meaningful, and which is something worth fighting to perpetuate. It also gives us the illusion of permanence without which the world would crumble into nihilistic anarchy.

The most powerful rituals are, however, social rituals – we act out something that expresses a common thread shared between us, and participating in the act reinforces a sense of belonging, a relief from isolation. Social ritual permeates our lives, through from football matches to débutante balls. When something good happens, or when we are smitten, we want to share it with others to give it meaning. Ritualised acts channel this desire and, by externalising it, make it real.

The great religions have mastered the power of ritual. They are amongst the most ritualised institutions to have ever appeared. Whether you are a Western churchgoer or not, the rituals espoused by the great religions will permeate your life – through from the great annual celebrations of Easter and Christmas to the way we handle death. None of us are as motivated by an abstract idea as we are by something tangible, something enacted. We are drawn to soaps about life's surreality, like *Ally McBeal*, more than we are to reading Jean-Paul Sartre. The process of enactment, of extemporisation, draws us in. For a moral order to be sustained it has to take on a form which compels us, which we can feel and which we can see acted out. The process of re-enactment reinforces meaning. That is why religion is full of ritualised enactments, of ceremony.

The Nation State is as ritualised an institution as religion. The process of state is enshrined in ritual, whether it be the swearing in of a new President or the stately banquets held for visiting state dignitaries. The visible forum of government, whether Parliament or the House of Representatives, is a theatre of ritualised debate and posturing. But more subtly, the society of every Nation State is characterised by ritualised social behaviour that sets the national character apart. In Spain the bullfight in the intense heat of a summer afternoon, where the blood smells with the intensity of ammonia, is an event as fundamental to the soul of the average Spanish male as is Catholicism. In America, the tail-gate barbecue at the Sunday game is a socialised rendition of the Indian gathering. In Britain, the excruciating gentlemanliness of cricket says something clear about the values of that small island. Ritual and the national character are inseparable. The Nation State is built upon them.

The by-product of such ritual is symbolism. Symbolism makes complex ideas concrete and thereby real. If they are concrete we can also control concepts that might otherwise overwhelm us. Whether we live in Kathmandu or Kentucky we all know, broadly speaking, what is signified by a crucifix or a five-pointed star, even if we are not versed in the doctrine underlying it. It connotes a meaning and describes a community of which we might or might not wish to be a part. The great religions have all turned the convoluted, abstract language of religious philosophy into a universalistic language of symbols, accessible and compelling even to the illiterates that comprise 40 per cent of the world's population. Their language is universally intelligible. The Nation State is also a master of symbolism. The Stars and Stripes or Union Jack are ingrained in every child's psyche, as are the anthems and formative allegorical figures from the past – from King Arthur through to Hiawatha. That ultimate expression of symbolism, language, crystallises the national identity. A national abroad can usually be identified within thirty seconds by a fellow national. The tattoos of nationality are indelible.

4. We all want to know where we come from. The Mormons' website on genealogy scores as many hits as any single part of Amazon. Historical continuity is a profound psychological need. We also need to believe we come from a good past that endorses our present. We all like to think well of our forebears. It is part of a healthy self-image. As a result, we tend to give great credence to the past. This may sound anachronistic in an age where change is meteoric and the past is dismissed as arcane by web-heads. But, psychologically, continuity is a foundation-stone of our sense of order. Our traditions make us secure. That is why, when push comes to shove, communities will defend them even to the death.

The evidence that something has worked in the past is also a powerful motivator. It brings the endorsement that this order has served generations before us – that it is not some dull contrivance. Tradition preserves what past generations have learnt and bequeaths it to the present as a blueprint for how to get by. It shows that what we are doing bears the proof of having served people before us who were better than us. It therefore gives us something to live up to, and to pass on.

The great religions have probably mastered the management of heritage more actively than any other institution. They define the history that gave rise to them. They enshrine a tradition that reassures us that we have a viable past, and that this is worth fighting for in order that we might bequeath it to our children. To prevent it wilting, they keep it alive through story-telling and fable. This past history is such a powerful motivator that, given the wrong circumstances, it has driven whole peoples to war to defend its traditions.

The Nation State has similarly swaddled itself in heritage. In fact, most people would be forgiven for assuming the Nation State had been around since time immemorial. As children we are all inculcated with a sense of our pastness. The study of history begins at age eight and from then on it forms an indelible part of what we are – the great sea battles, the national heroes, the revolutions, the forging of the state in blood and gore. The focuses of civic pride are usually museums. The greatest buildings are invariably state palaces.

As Howard Zinn suggests in his *People's History*, insecure regimes take the power of history so seriously that they usually reinvent it in a way that legitimises their role – something Stalin of course took to its insane extreme. As Confucius propounded, those nations that will ultimately succeed are those with the highest 'wen' – the most highly refined sense of their own culture. No country is more respectful of their past than the Chinese. But it is the almost obsessive reiteration of the cowboy motif that has perhaps made the US the king of the rose-tinted spectacles! It is a country hungry for history because it so obviously lacks one that is relevant to its deracinated population. In the absence of history you get Hollywood to invent it! An industry is born.

5. The need to ask, to satisfy our curiosity, is one of the most fundamental traits of human beings. Apparently, even our distant relatives – the chimpanzees – are more motivated to find out what is on the other side of a closed door than they are by the prospect of food or even sex! The process of questioning is closely bound up with a sense of progress, of optimism that there are things waiting to be found and which, through patient study, can ultimately be understood. The process of enquiry is, broadly speaking, synonymous with the process of human advancement. It was the Cartesian era of reason, the dismissal of creationist fatalism, that gave birth to scientific enquiry.

The great religions propound that there are important questions about purpose and meaning that we should not be afraid to ask. Religion tries to both arouse and point us in the direction of resolving the imponderable questions of where we come from, of what our role is on this earth. The process of asking is cathartic and invites the belief that, although imperfectly understood, there is a reason to the world if only we had the patience and clarity of mind to understand it. We continue asking and seeking because we trust that answers will ultimately be found and that the path is a rewarding one.

For a thousand years religious learning was the keystone of intellectual advancement. It is only relatively recently that the state educational system has assumed this mantle. Such questioning now actually threatens to discredit religious doctrine – how can anyone really turn water to wine and how can we therefore believe a word of it? But doctrine is not the same as the religion of which it is an interpretation at one point in time. Darwin has not answered the big question of the meaning of life. We continue to ask.

The democratic process of the Nation State places self-interrogation at its core. To the uninitiated, the vociferous debates in the chamber of the British Parliament can look almost infantile at times, and certainly chaotic. At the local level the intensity of debate is typically even more unbridled and unseemly. But it has its purpose. Fundamentally, democracy institutionalises the right to question the way things are done. That means that the political management process is continually evolving – new statutes are passed, old ones scrapped, faces change. Debate and dialogue infest all aspects of national society. It of course finds its mass outlet in the newspapers or, in the case of the UK in particular, in the infamous tabloids. For all the page three boobs and earthy epithets, the gutter press is the acme of any democracy!

It is the paralysis of debate, the quieting of the dissenting voice that marks the transition from democracy to totalitarianism. When the questions stop, so too does human progress. The interrogative mode of democracy is the best known path to advancement. That is why dirigist, conformist regimes, from Japan through to Korea, that stifle debate cannot sustain their momentum. They steadily decline and invite social revolution. Revolution occurs when regular change does not. The problem for business is that revolutions often mean receivership!

6. We all need to feel that there is something better we can strive for; that positive efforts will be positively rewarded. The absence of the possibility of self-improvement, whether morally or materially, ultimately saps any sense of drive, of optimism. People who, for whatever reason, are resigned to the status quo become fatalists. They lack life-force. Whether through forced retirement, social exclusion, classism or racism, the lack of the possibility of self-advancement is fundamentally debilitating. That is why, for the several hundred years there was feudalism in Europe, up until the Renaissance, nothing happened – it was literally a Dark Age. It is the resulting despair of exclusion among certain ethnic minorities that produces the social violence so familiar in many US cities.

The great religions ultimately take the view that good is on our side; that the future is worth fighting for however bad the present. They stringently reject passivity, fatalism, and resignation – the three most corrosive forces that stunt productivity. The great religions militate for advancement, for hope. Judaism in particular – perhaps the most influential force in Western thought – sides firmly with the underdog and proposes a philosophy of self-betterment. It propounds that there is something worth getting out of bed to battle for each day.

The democratic basis of the modern Nation State is built around a dynamic of self-improvement. The prime measure of economic competitiveness is GNP per capita – an implicit acknowledgement that a prime role of the state is to enhance the material well-being of its citizens. At its core the taxation process is about reallocation of resources to improve the average lot. The political process itself, founded on representation, enshrines the principle that everyone's voice can ultimately be heard. The law is there to defend that right, to level the playing-field. The Nation State gives us the framework to drag ourselves up – to invent ourselves. It also provides a base-line below which it is hard to sink unless you try really hard. But it is only through participation that improvement is possible.

Perhaps the most optimistic Nation State of them all is, of course, the United States. The American Dream is a national institution. Legislation is, partially at least, crafted to accommodate it – from comparatively benign bankruptcy laws to low capital gains tax. It is an entirely legitimate expectation to attend Harvard and make a million as a second-generation citizen. National society provides the ladder and social expectations set the incentive. To belong you must excel. It is an expectant nation.

7. We all appear to have a profound need for mystery, to believe that there are forces that we can only dimly understand. That there is more out there than we can possibly grasp. If the world was completely intelligible, if there wasn't the promise of things we have not yet seen, then it would indeed be a dull place. There would be no room for advancement, no room for revelation, no room for redemption. The existence of mystery is closely bound up with optimism and positivism. In the absence of satisfactory mystery, we invent it. Recognising the limits of our abilities to perceive, to comprehend, is essential in order to assure us that there is no limit to how far we can go – should we be smart enough.

The great religions cloak themselves in mystery. Their origins are opaque; their progenitors miracle workers; their vision less than accessible. Their pervasive use of symbolism and ritual in place of terse statement of fact reinforces the ambiguity. In a world which is brutally simple in terms of material power, this ambiguity leaves a space for redemption, where there is the possibility of something wonderful happening. That's what keeps us going!

The reason we all tend to believe that the Nation State is older than it is, is partly for the same reason – that its origins are embroidered with mystery. The Arthurian legend in England, the semi-biblical progress of Washington across the Delaware river, the chameleon qualities of the loveable tyrant Napoleon, all are elements of the national myth – the myth that we as peoples are born of mystical, semi-divine events. Unless our origins are somehow otherworldly, then it is hard believing that the structures imposed by society have any ultimate validity. It was precisely these powers that were invoked by monarchs seeking to consolidate their position through the myth of kingship by divine right. Divine right has been displaced by democracy but the need for myth has not gone with it. The speeches of Churchill that invoke the Haraldian past still stir the British heart.

Towards a corporate heartland

There are four great societal institutions in the lives of Western society – the Nation State, the Church, family, and the place of work. Over the course of the fifty or so years since the Second World War, the relative importance of them to our daily lives has shifted dramatically. The family has been eroded by social mobility – in many ways a good thing, of course. The Church as an institution has declined. Finally, as we shall come on to, the relevance of the Nation State is being called into question by the counter-forces of economic integration and political devolution.

We talked earlier in this chapter about the evolution of the Nation State from its old elitist form towards a representative

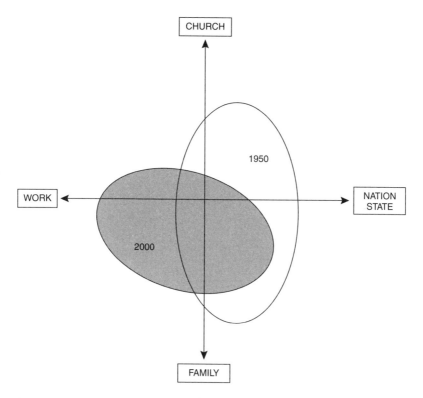

Figure 3.2   The relative importance of the key social forces in our daily lives

framework. The fact is, however, that most political regimes have not yet fully achieved the conversion from the old state to the new. The case of the majority of Third World coun-tries is clear and does not need to be reiterated. However, even in the case of developed countries, there is often a subtle failure to fully espouse modern political management. The most obvious manifestation is an enduring obsession with protecting the interests of producers rather than those of consumers. Partly this is based on innocent error – the belief that, if national business is not protected, then jobs will be

lost and social inequality grow. But partly it is a function of
the vested interests of an elite whose lobbying power is con-
siderable with relatively underpaid politicians. What began
in many cases with social modernisation, has ended with
defence of inefficient national industry, the only remedy to
which is privatisation. French politicians still find that a hard
pill to swallow.

But even where the political process has successfully
evolved from old to new, the foundation of the social contract
is being disrupted by the increased mobility of both people
and ideas. The social contract can no longer rely on a static
cultural affinity between state and people. Indians in Bradford
are as British as Welsh coalminers in Llandudno. But is a
Basque also Spanish? Does a Catalan owe fealty to Madrid?
All over the Western world the cultural basis of the contract
between citizen and state is being called into question. The
potency of these changes is reflected in the reactionism of
those threatened by it, whether Le Pen in France, Buchanan
in the US or John Howard in Australia. During his defeat
of Keating in the 1996 election campaign, Howard famously
charged that Australians were losing their national icons and
even their sovereignty to the global market. Even predominantly Europhile Blair has slowed the rate of the UK's entry
into the Euro because of the same xenophobic national sentiment amongst many voters.

That leaves our place of work, or for the 24 per cent of
us who work for companies with more than five thousand
employees, the corporation. That is the primary social institution of the four and where we increasingly invest our
emotional lives. The average knowledge worker puts in a 60-
hour week and the emotional investment is even greater. The
workplace has de facto become a key social institution in our
lives. The only problem is that few companies have actually

recognised that fact and virtually none have turned it to their advantage. They are unwittingly and often reluctantly becoming social constructs.

We have noted that the qualities that have made religion and the Nation State such enduring and potent social forces appear to be common to both of them. But what is equally surprising is how poorly these heartland qualities appear to be understood. Despite the vast reams of consultancy material produced annually on strategy, none of these phenomena appear to have been systematically applied in the context of the corporation. Formal corporate strategy, originally enunci-ated by Michael Porter, has virtually nothing to say about any of the seminal characteristics we have observed. That is an extraordinary fact! It is particularly extraordinary given the fact that countries and corporations in many fundamental ways mirror each other – as we should expect them to do given they are both forms of social organisation. But that is another chapter of our story!

4

State versus corporation: identifying the common genes

We have talked of corporations and states as if they were completely different types of social organisation. In fact, state and corporation in many ways mirror each other in their organisational characteristics – even though most CEOs and corporate strategists would shudder to think of their firms having commonality with political states. In fact, the bonds are there, only no-one seems to have noticed! They may be different beasts but they have the same DNA. These commonalities have important implications when it comes to transposing the lessons of the Nation State onto the society of the global firm.

The state management models

All modern Western states are profoundly influenced by the
Bretton Woods foundation, embodying the principle that
government should regulate markets to prevent abuses and
guarantee international free trade. Within this broad context
there are three dominant models of political–economic
organisation:

- The Anglo-Saxon shareholder and open capital markets
  system.
- The Germano-Japanese oligopolistic nationalist system.
- The Franco-Italian statist system.

The Anglo-Saxon system dominates the modern business
mindset, fuelled by the MBA phenomenon and dominance
of US business practices. It is, as we all know, characterised
by the pre-eminence of the shareholder. The role of government is simply to ensure a viable but usually innocuous
regulatory environment (although instances such as the battle
with Microsoft over browser software shows how the state
can have regulatory teeth – and sharp ones at that!) and to
provide a safety-net to pick up those people who can't cut
it in the open employment market. The state in principle
plays second fiddle to the corporate community and the
stock market. Beyond indirect control of interest rates and
government spending, perhaps its single most critical role is
the provision of educational infrastructure. The ancillary,
although not inconsequential, obligation is the provision of
national defence. Most people reading this book will almost
certainly take this system of management for granted.
However, although it is ever increasingly the dominant one,

the Anglo-Saxon shareholder-centric model is not the only show in town.

The Germano-Japanese system raises enterprise as a national goal and one to preoccupy policy makers. The state bureaucracy is charged with actively promoting growth and targeted investment. This is usually delivered by private enterprises but those that are often bound together by common equity bonds and command an oligopolistic position in the national market which is tacitly endorsed by officials. The state plays a crucial role in controlling the debt markets and also regulating the labour market. The result is a corporate environment of intense elitism based on close political ties and with minimal levels of disclosure of information to the markets. This makes these markets fiendish labyrinths for foreign competitors to try to penetrate. For the same reason, FDI to these markets tends to be minimal. Typically the equity markets are comparatively underdeveloped and subject to government policy.

The third dominant model, the statist model, moves the state bureaucracy centre stage. The Ministry of Finance is the dominant force shaping the corporate world, regulating capital markets directly. The flow of senior people between senior corporate and bureaucratic positions is almost seamless. Advancement comes through preferment. Elitism and cultural xenophobia are the by-product. Public enterprise adamantly resists privatisation and relies on tacit forms of protectionism and favourable financing to preserve its oligopoly. Entrepreneurialism is a comparative rarity and labour rigidity is profound. The elite enjoys snails and fine claret; the workers enjoy job stability, although that is usually not what they end up with, of course, as global competition inevitably kicks in.

As recently as the early 1990s the Germano-Japanese

model was, as amazing as it may now seem, in the ascendant
and the Anglo-Saxon model was at a nadir. Then by 1995
the tables had firmly reversed as inflation dropped and the
philosophy of share ownership began to take hold. Major
corporations began to detach themselves from their national
political minders to free their own hands. By 1997 Japan had
emerged as a bankrupt system unable to manage its own
finances and, under the weight of reunification, Germany had
by 1992 already begun to show serious signs of slowing. More
fundamentally, highly xenophobic corporations began to
appear sorely inept at dealing with a changing environment,
having been saddled with regulated workforces, inflexible
working practices, bank debt and myopic management. By
March 2000 the unthinkable happened – the proud German
telco Mannesman succumbed to a hostile bid from the UK's
Vodafone.

The corporate management models

The above three generic models of national management are
mirrored by the three dominant models of global corporate
management, namely:

- The US centrist federalist model
- The European subsidiarity model
- The Germano-Japanese global monolith model

American corporations are typified by what can best be termed
centralised federalism, exemplified in all the archetypal US
giants, from GM, P&G and Coke through to the likes of IBM.
All have expanded into international markets based on the
size and wealth of their home market, their overseas sub-

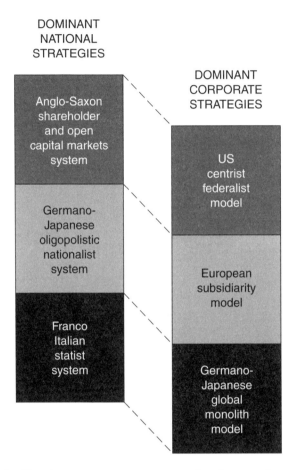

Figure 4.1   Dominant corporate versus national strategies

sidiaries exploiting and marketing products first tried and tested in the US. International subsidiaries operate with reasonable autonomy when it comes to matters of marketing and local sales relationships. But all the core value added in terms of R&D and new product development remains firmly in the hands of the US-based top management, along with all interaction with the dominant institutional shareholding base. Corporate strategy is a US affair, which also explains why US academic institutions have a virtual monopoly of thinking in this area.

US corporations have, of course, closely mirrored the political evolution of their home market. The US is a federation and the Founding Fathers ensured a separation of power between the legislature, executive and judiciary. But after the Civil War centralising forces established an equal influence and were later reinforced by the New Deal which established the primacy of the Federal Government in driving economic policy. Despite the gradual encroachment of the concept of Union, Europe has by contrast remained a federation of much looser sort than its cousin across the Pond.

The major European corporations, although far smaller in number and more diminutive then their US cousins, tend to mirror the political structure of their own regional market. Whether Philips, Unilever or Nestlé, local subsidiaries tend to be highly independent of the centre. Scale economies are generally sacrificed in favour of being highly responsive to local tastes. Production tends to be customised to the local market, and brands are dominantly national, rather than global. That is why European brands rarely cut the mustard in the US.

Unlike the US centrist federalists, the European federalists tend to have large central bureaucracies, necessary to administer a complex network of local relationships. They also tend to be far more sensitised to political relationships with local state elites. Broadly speaking, as a consequence, European corporates have done better in Europe than their US rivals in sectors where local customisation is more valued, such as foodstuffs, professional services, fashion and aspects of media. That is also what has made good firms in these sectors such appetising acquisition targets for Americans such as P&G!

The structure of the Germano-Japanese monoliths has similarly mirrored the dominant political model of their home market. Whether Matsushita, Toyota, Sony, Deutschebank or Mercedes Benz, they have sought global dominance in their chosen markets by achieving scale in their home market and then extending it globally. It is growth by cloning. Their overseas operations are ostensibly export operations, staffed by minions from Tokyo or Munich. Corporate strategy is strictly a top-down affair and autonomy throughout the global network is minimal. Production is largely done at home where scale economies and automation are the tenets of competitive advantage. The associated producers' mentality is genetic.

Of course, no model is static. The dominant US and European models have evolved over time in line with their respective political economies. As we have already discussed, from 1918 to the mid-1970s, Western governments assumed responsibility for managing their national economies to a degree they never had before. The evolving corporate giants mirrored the same characteristics, of governance through strict top-down management. It was in this era of centrism that corporate strategy was born – not unanalogous to the growth in military strategy.

But by 1985 this had firmly begun to change. The key trigger was the spectacular resurgence of free-market liberal democracy. As Thatcher and Reagan began to slim down government, the same process unfolded amongst corporate bureaucracies. It was the era of downsizing, reengineering and rightsizing. The inevitable corollary in the political sphere was the growth in political autonomy of regions, from Wales through to the Basque country. In the corporate sphere, the balance between federalism and centrism tipped in favour of the former. The regional manager began to come to the fore. The concept of subsidiarity took firm hold, reinforced by the shift of added value to marketing and away from production. Market sensitivity or differentiation began to eclipse the quest for scale economies or low-cost strategies as a source of competitive advantage.

Most firms continue to face the dilemma of whether to preserve the more comfortable approach of centrism, or swallow hard and allow subsidiarity. Often this boils down to a choice of whether to export or whether to develop a local market presence. The problem with an export strategy is that it is vulnerable to exchange rate shifts, to tariffs and to the vagaries of international transport costs. The mercantilist struggle for market share in industrial exports from a compact national base in the traditional Germano-Japanese model is increasingly less viable. The growth in the service and marketing element of all consumption makes localisation a virtual sine qua non. Even the major web players have found it necessary to localise their sites and to use local URLs such as .co.uk or .fr. As Percy Barnevik of ABB famously put it in the *Harvard Business Review*, 'You have to have deep local roots everywhere you operate – building products where you sell them, recruiting the best local talent from universities, working with the local government to increase exports.' On the other hand, of course, FDI has its political perils. A corporation's bargaining power with government erodes as it takes root in local soil and the costs of exit rise. Choices, choices . . . !

Cutting the national umbilical cord

The fact that companies have historically mimicked the organisational characteristics of their home countries should not be surprising. Corporations have not been consciously shaped as viable long-term social units. As a result they have simply mirrored the domestic society from which they originate. Most so-called global corporations are in fact the progeny of national political forces. Most fundamental to the development of the corporate landscape in the West was the Allied victory in 1945 that paved the way for the dominance of US corporations in Europe and the global spread of US business practices. The profound limitation with all three corporate models is that they still make the nation, and particularly the home nation, the central pillar of their guiding philosophy.

The big question therefore is, is it really in a corporation's interests to be so bound to the political evolution of their dominant markets? Particularly, as we will explore in the next chapter, at a time when the Nation State as an institution appears to be losing a degree of its relevance to educated populations? What is the benefit of unshackling themselves? For a firm to evolve globally, it has to be founded on a community that is bigger than, and distinct from, the society of the Nation State in which it grew up. The analogy with the adult discovery of self-identity is a valid one. No-one, not even an institution like a firm, can discover its own identity without abandoning the security of the nest. To achieve statehood, the firm needs to establish its own society, distinct from that of its home market. But an important part of that process is learning the social lessons of the state. To grow up you first have to learn the tricks of your parents!

5

The state of the Nation State: opportunity or threat?

Although they control 40 per cent of economic activity, things are not all rosy for the politicians in their marbled hallways of state. The Nation State is seen by many illustrious commentators to be losing relevance. The state would appear to be an institution caught between two seismic forces that threaten to tear it apart:

- Consolidation of countries into regional blocks driven by economic forces of globalisation.
- Fragmentation of countries into regional sub-nations based on ethnic and political lines.

In essence, the forces tugging the Nation State in opposite directions differ little from those faced by the nascent global

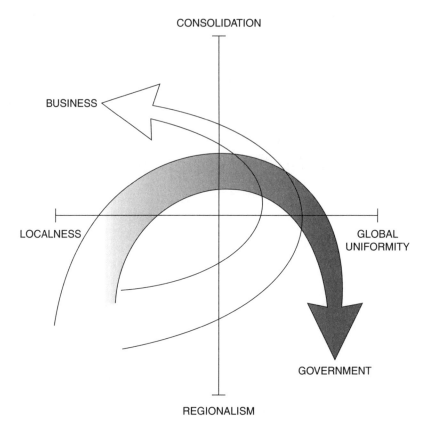

Figure 5.1 The evolving orientation of business versus government

company – the economic imperative to consolidate and acquire, in order to achieve scale, versus the natural frag-mentation of businesses into local operating units with quasi-autonomous management. We have proposed the Nation State as a model of social management but this doesn't seem an auspicious beginning. Is there a viable strategy to accom-modate both forces and, if so, what is it? Can the firm learn from the management processes of the state? Let's examine both forces in turn.

Economic consolidation: from nation to block

The past twenty years have seen the increasing shift of economic power to large trading blocks, from Mercosur, NAFTA, the EC, to the Danish–Swedish Oresund. Trade, foreign investment and currency flows have grown at many times the rate of national economies. After Nixon's announcement in 1971 of the end of convertibility, global daily trade in foreign exchange shot from $15 billion in 1973 to $1,300 billion by 1995. This is equivalent to a hundred times the average daily turnover of trade in physical goods. The government-centred design for the world created at Bretton Woods was officially ended with the freeing of short-term capital flows and German unity in 1990. FDI grew fourfold between 1990 and 1993, stabilising at $145 billion in 1994 and then soaring to $245 billion in 1996. This represented around 4 per cent of the combined economies of the developing world. In addition, by 1996 sales by all foreign affiliates had exceeded the world total of exports of goods and services.

The effect of trade, and particularly regional trade, has been to erode the economic distinctions between national markets. To the economist's mind, borders represent friction and friction reduces margins. The economist's imperative, therefore, is to consolidate and harmonise. In relative terms, that is precisely what has happened over the past twenty years. In 1850 China was a mysterious landmass seduced into Western trade with opium. By the 1990s it had become the outsourced production centre for every variety of Western plastic consumer good imaginable, from hairbrushes to Superman icons.

The secondary effect of global capital flows has been to extend the reach of liberal economics to a new set of national players. Emerging markets have come to represent 10 per cent of total global capitalisation, 80 per cent of which is controlled and created by private rather than government money, with corporate investment representing about 40 per cent of the total.

The globalisation of financial markets has eroded the post-war assumption that governments should manage their national economies. The Bretton Woods accord stipulated that, if one country began to run permanent surpluses or deficits on trade, the rate of exchange of its currency relative to others would be negotiated in the IMF and between governments to redress the balance. Currencies were ultimately fixed based on a gold price of $35 per ounce. Unregulated markets were not regarded as trustworthy. Such regulation is, of course, anathema to contemporary economics which is premised on deregulated markets. The old equation that local savings and investment are mutually interdependent no longer holds true.

The explosion in tradable financial instruments has profound implications for governments accustomed to paddling their own canoes. National economic performance can now be judged in the Forex markets. The efficacy of government political management can be assessed in the Bond markets. The verdict of risk assessment agencies such as Moody's and Standard and Poor's now has a profound bearing on the cost of government money. No country can run its economy entirely independently of its neighbours.

That missing ingredient – politics

As early as 1748 Montesquieu had observed presciently, 'The state of things in Europe is that all the states depend on each other. Europe is a single state comprised of several provinces . . .'. Two hundred years on we have come full circle. But the surrender of a degree of economic authority to larger trading blocks has not been met with a corresponding transfer of political authority. If anything, political power has been

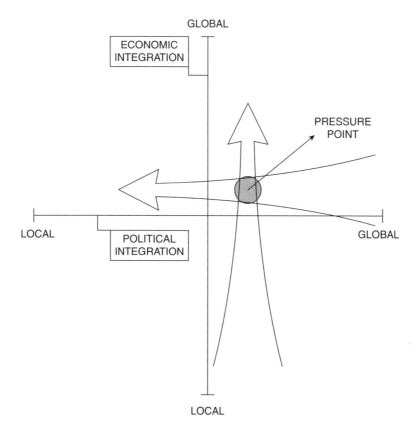

Figure 5.2 The forces of economic versus political integration

dramatically devolved since the Second World War. In 1946 the United Nations had 51 members, today it has three times that number and growing.

One fundamental problem with political as opposed to economic integration is that the governing principles behind different states differ radically. The UK and Scandinavia, for example, operate under Common Law. France, Germany and southern Europe, by contrast, operate under the Napoleonic Code. In Common Law the individual is permitted to do anything that is not specifically prohibited. Under the Napoleonic Code the law establishes individual obligation. These legalistic differences are one formal expression of fundamental cultural gulfs between peoples, of which political ambitions are a manifestation.

In an age dominated by global econ-speak, it is easy to forget that politics dictate the interaction of societies. Thinking that national politics no longer mattered would be a terrible mistake. The case of Japan illustrates that it is not simply economic virility that drives global position. Japan's political backwardness and intense introversion have now begun to erode its ability to function. But, more broadly, without the appropriate political framework global economic forces would evaporate.

The lack of trust between states sets keen limits to their readiness to depend on world markets. The name of the game beyond security is still to ensure that their own producers win more market access. There is a dense web of interconnectedness between political objectives and those of national producers. Overcoming this axiomatic social agenda is extremely tough, as the faltering beginnings of the Euro has demonstrated. It is not for nothing that the men in history who have come nearest to establishing an international order have been pleasant fellows like Alexander,

Caesar, Charlemagne and Napoleon. Napoleon was defeated by a coalition of powers who for the first time formally assumed the status of great powers and committed to govern Europe by congress. It was this reconquest by force that actually gave birth to the concept of Europe as a political system. But, in all practicality, it has not actually evolved much further in the intervening two hundred years.

The key political wills of states have been kept in check for the last fifty years by a balance of power, not by covenants or international institutions. It still takes the Hobbesian leviathan to tame greed and instil fear. As soon as a dominant power achieves the possibility of regional domination, history has shown they tend to rise to the bait. The period between 1914 and 1945 was amongst the most unstable in the world's history because of the unequal distribution of power. Interestingly, this was at exactly the same time that political philosophers were beginning to apply Darwinist analysis to politics and to contemplate power in geopolitical terms. If the opportunity to achieve decisive political competitive advantage exists, it typically is indeed taken. The period from the 1890s to the 1940s was one of rapidly changing disparities in the effective strength of the major powers. By contrast, since 1945 the distribution of power has generally been more stable than it has been at any time since 1902. Hence the illusion of a new world of impartial market forces presided over by an invisible hand.

In an age that appears to be economically driven, human concerns and their medium, politics, still hold the dominant hand. Our world market is still driven by politics and politics are the domain of the Nation State. Were Russia to crumble into militaristic anarchy, were China to retreat into ideology, were Germany to retreat from European union under pressure from the Freedom Party, then the so-called global market would very abruptly be stopped in its tracks. The spread of market democracy provides no surety of indefinite worldwide peace. Fundamentally, it is underpinned by the US and, as soon as Washington retreats for whatever domestic reason, the world trade market will also, followed by deflation of global stock-markets. So the timescale for making a sweeping judgement that Nation States will not return to the squabbling of the 1850s is too limited. Their recent behaviour has been conditioned by the unique bipolar freeze of the cold war.

That is a lesson understood by the US, which continues to sustain an international policy despite the cost. But only as long as the US considers that world trade is in its best interests will it sustain global markets. If it fears that others are making gains at its own expense then the US will withdraw its sponsorship of the system. The same holds true for the global political institutions such as the UN. The UN would have been as impotent in Kosovo as it was in Kuwait without direct US military support. Whilst the US continues to drag its feet over payment of its UN dues, its tacit support of the liberal internationalising ideology the UN represents is what keeps that institution going. Realpolitik is alive and kicking, even if it now wears an Armani suit!

Integration that is possible on an economic basis is ultimately thwarted in vanquishing the world in some Ricardian Wall Street utopia by political and social fragmentation. The emerging pattern is an ambivalent one of regional economic integration offset by political devolution. One satisfies the hunger for efficiency, the other feeds on the deep-rooted social instincts we all share.

Political fragmentation: from nation to local region

The impetus for political devolution has increased dramatically over the past twenty years. The 51 territories that were signatories to the UN charter at San Francisco in 1945 had swollen to 185 by 1990. The principle of self-determination enshrined in the UN charter had fragmented the global market-place as much as it had liberated it. By the 1970s OPEC had thrown off the mantle of economic imperialism and extended Arab ownership over their natural resources. The stage was set for everyone else to follow suit. The defining force behind the seismic shift is, of course, ethnicity – the fundamental definition of who we are and where we come from.

Increasingly the unit of political relevance, at least on a par with the state, is the region. Were Vasco da Gama to peer over the shoulders of a modern cartographer he would now see a world map equally as fractured as back in 1496. In Germany much political power has been ceded to the Länder. In Canada Quebec has become de facto independent. In Spain an explicit policy of devolution has transferred much of the apparatus of statehood to the country's autonomous communities such as Pais Vasco and Catalonia. In Italy the Lombard League is a major force for casting the leaking ship of the Mezzogiorno adrift into the Med. France's 22 provinces have significant political clout even against a backdrop of Gaullist dirigism. The tech-heads of the Bay Area in Northern California or the entrepreneurs of Guangdong in Southern China regard themselves as distinct entities from their host nations. Groupings based on culture and civilisation are proving as compelling as allegiances based on nationhood and perhaps more so than those based on economics. The battles of Hutu and Tutsi in Rwanda are a painful reminder of that fact.

Nations and their politicians do not fully represent these real markets. The United Nations' 185 delegates do not represent Hong Kong or Silicon Valley, or Palestine or Catalonia. Economic and social modernisation has to an extent begun to separate people from their long-standing identification with the state and to cast them back to their religious and cultural roots. Such cultural identification cannot be discarded like ideologies. Nor does it rise and fall like economic fortunes. The conflagration of wars in the quagmire of ex-Yugoslavia is testimony to this fact. The severity of fighting in Lebanon and the West Bank shows that the decades where consumerism marketised the economy do not make older cultural fault lines obsolete. The slings and arrows still let fly.

The most relevant sphere of most people's lives is either local or regional. People increasingly want local representation and accountability. As a result, economic power and political representation have inevitably grown apart. The resurgence of regional languages has been dramatic over the past twenty years for a good reason. The real question is, if political units remain fundamentally local, will not global integration be stalled in its tracks? After all, there are around 30 or so regional states that are probably of more interest to global corporations than the rest of the world's Nation States combined.

Stepping amongst stumbling giants

So what does this all add up to? The Nation State is the key nexus of social cohesion. But it is entering a period of schizo-

phrenia between the competing forces of ethnic fragmentation and the globalisation of economic markets. Indeed, as
political pressures intensify and localise, so conflict with
global market forces is also likely to harden.

States will to some degree at least lose their relevance.
The liberalisation programmes of the EU and GATT have
threatened states' leverage over their own financial systems.
In the new bipolar world of the EU and the US which has
replaced the balance of the cold war, power is increasingly
regionally centralised and regions' respective nations or states
look increasingly like subsidiaries. At the same time ethnic
enclaves are gaining momentum and dividing the political
units of nations. These statelets tend to be politically motivated units. There are instances of solely economic units such
as Silicon Valley and Guangdong. But the majority are
inspired by the cultural and political instincts of autonomy.
The response to these pressures at the country level is the
inevitable rise of nationalism, invoked by politicians whose
role in society could so easily be whittled away to nothing.

Economic forces are compelling corporations to expand
and compete globally at exactly the same time as the tides
of nationalism are rising once again worldwide. The most
acute nexus of this lies in the protection of jobs. Part of the
issue lies in the fact that governments globally have been
slow to grasp that their roles have subtly changed from being
the protector of their people and their natural resources from
outside economic and military threats, to ensuring that their
people have the widest choice of goods possible. The Nation
State becomes, in e-parlance, a portal. Although current
consumption patterns persist in being local, the driving force
is towards far less consumer concern for where goods come
from. The relevance of national taste is an industry in sharp
decline. Indeed national taste is often now simply a political

tool. The furore in Europe over BSE-contaminated beef was a startling illustration of how politics could co-opt the call to national sentiment for political gain.

Nationalism has become an unfashionable term. But it is still the strongest beast on the playing-field. The rise of liberalism in the early 1900s freed people from state religion and allowed them the choice of pursuing their own religion as long as they did no harm to others. This fostered the spread of secularism with its attendant sense of loss and alienation. Into this void stepped Hitler and Mussolini. Most of us in the West are liberal internationalists. But it is easy to assume wrongly that these values are universally shared and to underestimate the appeal of nationalism, particularly to non-Western peoples.

It is an easy assumption that the spread of liberal democracy of the past twenty years is a one-way street to nirvana. The past should tell us to be wary of such blithe assumptions. In an important sense the 1990s have mirrored the years prior to 1914. In both periods trade witnessed a steady expansion, with a boom in primary product exports. Industrial investment flourished, financed through corporate equity and government bonds. A world financial market was conceived between London, Paris and Berlin. Norman Angell expressed the prevailing sentiment of the time in his 1910 book *The Great Illusion*, 'International finance is now so interdependent and tied to trade and industry that military and political power can in reality do nothing.' How wrong he was!

In the vortex of shifting horizons one thing is for certain – the one world that Roberto Goizueta envisaged in the 1980s is very far from being a reality. Whilst the financial markets have partly fulfilled his vision, politically nothing much has progressed. And it is politics that drives society. The world straddled by the global corporation is a mosaic of competing and divergent social interests. And large corporations have far less negotiating power with these units than is commonly supposed. Large corporations provide 80 per cent of value added and exports in advanced industrial countries. But they only provide 35 per cent of the jobs. To political entities it is people that matter. The days of the Hudson Bay Company and East India Company are gone.

What does this mean for the corporation?

The CEO cannot rely on one-world economics to oil her path. The corporation can either find itself crushed in the tectonic plates of rival political processes, or alternatively carve out its own social identity to balance that of the statal societies with which it interacts. In so doing, the corporation has an opportunity to play a greater societal role which will fundamentally change its competitiveness. As we explored in Chapter 3, there has always been a tension between the four dominant institutions in everyone's life, and the firm has historically been in the weakest position. There is now an opportunity to change that. The fact is the firm has little choice, if it is to achieve sustainable differentiation on a global basis. Strategy has to be social strategy or it is no strategy at all.

6

Founding the corporate state: laying the philosophical foundations

Capitalism and democracy have traditionally obeyed different principles. In capitalism wealth, and particularly wealth of shareholders, has been the objective. In democracy the objective has been political authority. In capitalism the unit of account is money; in a democracy it is the citizen's vote.

On this basis, the popular imagination pits the large corporation and the Nation State into ambivalent opposition. The Nation State posits itself as the defender of employee interests and guardian of its national market. The corporation assumes the fight of the shareholder, and espouses the cause of the customer irrespective of which market they live in. The electorate is pitted against the shareholder, and each is pushed into dichotomous alignment with the Nation State and the company respectively.

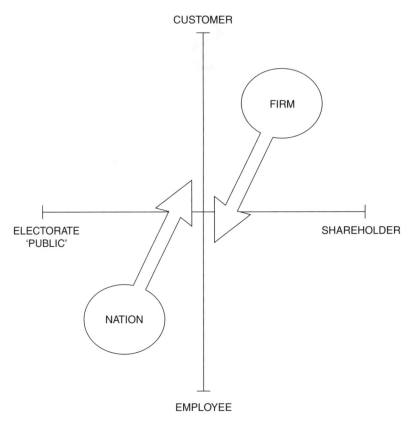

Figure 6.1 The changing strategic focus of firms versus governments

There is no particularly sound reason for this conflictual position but the fact is it is very real. As long as it remains so, scenes such as the recent one at the UK BMW plant in Longbridge will be repeated. Corporations need to understand their relationship with their own people as citizens of the corporate society they work in. Conversely, the state needs to understand its role in protecting the interests of the consumer, rather than focusing on defending the viability of national producers.

For these things to come to pass, the corporation needs inevitably to look more like a state, or to be precise, a corporate state. That means one serious sea change – corporations must recognise that they are social structures and that their competitiveness resides principally in their ability to manage their own societies. Achieving competitive advantage hinges firstly on people and secondly on efficiency, not the other way around! As corporations seek to globalise, to break their national ties, the issue of what constitutes the heartland of their society will become more acute. How do you make ten thousand talented people scattered across the globe feel commitment and allegiance to a company when their principle social context is where they live? It is pretty clear that most firms are not good at it. They die young – age 40. They also find it impossible to break the umbilical links to the nest – they rarely grow up into mature social structures! There is a whole side to the development of the firm that has been overlooked by corporate strategy. The philosophical foundation of statehood requires making that shift to social self-recognition.

Rediscovering the human factor

The conditions necessary for the corporation to assume a position of greater social importance are all there, as the other competing dimensions of society – church, family and state – are in relative decline. The Nation State, which has historically been the principal social unit, is, as we have explored, under pressure from economic forces beyond its control. Its relevance to a society characterised by devolution is arguably declining. National economies also have to a significant degree been overtaken by the global economy. But the global economy is no real substitute. It is not a fifth social dimen-sion of our model.

The global economy does share a common trading currency – the dollar – which enables it to function effec-tively. But what this international web does not possess is a set of common values. It has no common legal or ethical framework. As a consequence it operates in an entirely trans-actional fashion based on price information. It does not operate like a conventional market – based on relationships. That means it has no capacity to act as a social medium. The replacement of relationships by transactions has been an ongoing process throughout history. But growth in currency trading, and the explosion of trading mediums such as the Internet, have accelerated this in the last decade. The result is music to the economist's ears – an increasingly frictionless playing-field devoid of human peculiarity. But what there is not is a viable global political system to manage it.

The global system cannot supplant the national one which is based on social values. A globalised market can never satisfy our need for belonging. It must always remain something abstract. The result is a dialectic between an ever-developing global transactional market and a frag-menting regional market based on social relationships. The economic and social processes are moving in opposite direc-tions.

The opportunity for the corporate state is to bring them back into line – to respond to the global challenge of seam-less international trade, by creating a viable global society to support that process. This would deliver immense competi-tive advantage to the firm that could achieve it – a globally motivated workforce operating to similar values would be unstoppable. The question is how to do so? We have explored how the Nation State, like that other great set of social institutions, the religions, actually holds some important lessons about developing cohesive societies. It is these lessons that we must assimilate into the business arena. For it is the ability to create a cohesive society that will drive the competitiveness of the aspiring global firm.

The foundation stone: creating a corporate society

In *Reinspiring the Corporation*, we described the creation of a coherent, motivated firm as 'reinspiration' – literally animating people to act together to achieve something great. The analogy we used was the building of Chartres Cathedral. Corporate reinspiration is founded on the notion of 'community'. A community is the social bedrock necessary before people can share values and act coherently. A community is bound together by a shared identity. Communities turn individual energy into pooled energy capable of moving mountains. Without a sense of community, a group of people will be torpid, ineffectual and not really constitute a group at all.

Modern communities tend to be more dispersed culturally and geographically then they ever were historically. Communities also tend to have fuzzy edges. They are not as clearly defined as a club or a tribe. People drift in and out, sometimes leaving for a while, only to return much later in their lives. Communities also tend to tolerate fairly diverse groups of people, sometimes comprised of ethnic subgroups which may vary from each other quite dramatically. Perhaps the most extreme contemporary expressions of the concept of community are the popular special interest sites on the Internet. Geocities calls itself a community – a community of people spread across the globe, the vast majority of whom will never interact with their fellow members other than through a wire and screen.

The concept of community is a powerful but troubled one in the corporate context. Corporate communities, like social communities, have changed dramatically. The inexorable process of globalisation amongst most of the larger firms has meant that they can no longer rely on social commonality conditioned by where they happen to be headquartered. The IBM occupying an entire Midwestern town no longer dictates the basis of social cohesion of that firm. This umbilical linkage to the larger society of the region or state is eroding rapidly and corporations are currently the losers. You only have to look at the average rate of executive churn.

The modern firm faces the challenge of trying to corral peoples dispersed across dozens of countries into some coherent 'culture'. Around 55 per cent of the Fortune 500's manufacturing is now done by overseas subsidiaries. The strain on the traditional definition of community has never been greater. The necessary transition is from locally defined community to international society. A robust society can accommodate multiple communities, but bound together within a coherent framework, much as the society of the state accommodates communities as distinct as Cockney milkmen and Welsh coalminers or Apache Indians and German Mennonites.

From employee to citizen

The key ingredient in making the leap from a local community to a mature society is the concept of citizenship. The contract between employee and firm is based on work and reward. It is typically a linear relationship. The task is fairly prescribed and financial reward correlates directly to it. Titles denote position in the hierarchy. The flow of authority is clearly one way. By contrast, the contract between citizen and state is very different. It supposes a reciprocal relationship with a set of social anchors at its core that nourish and validate the relationship. These range from the right to vote and the obligation to pay taxes, through to the acceptance of a shared view of morality, upheld by the judicial process. A wide range of emotional benefits is to be received in return for commitment to the process.

Citizenship based on social participation is fundamentally distinct from the usual characteristics of the employee–employer relationship. Within the corporate world, probably the closest analogy is the partnership structure of the professional service firm. But partnership structures are not viable in businesses where capital is deployed and which therefore need access to public markets. Behind the concept of citizenship lies a set of factors that conditions the citizen–state relationship, which can be more readily assimilated by the company. It is these that can be emulated to energise the relationship between firm and employee that lies at the heart of the corporate community:

1   A framework of moral authority that binds the society of the firm together behind a unified purpose. Everyone party to it feels infused with a virtuous ambition to propagate the firm's way of doing things. The correct path is clear, even if it is not without its immense challenges.

2   An environment that obviates the need for continual self-questioning and allows for close identification with group interests. No-one is eaten by self-doubt or reservations about what they are doing. The task is clear and it is shared. Participation in it is exhilarating.

Figure 6.2 Factors conditioning the citizen–state relationship that can be assimilated by the firm

3   Absolute clarity of identity. There is no mistaking the firm in any of its manifestations. To the members of the society of the firm, its identity is a rich, cohesive language that connotes a like-minded way of thinking amongst its citizens – even if it sometimes results in aggressive debate. Participation in that language provides self-validation.

4   A keen sense by the society of the firm of where it has come from and what it stands for. Participation in shaping that heritage into the future lends all citizens a level of purpose, a reason to strive to propagate the society, which perhaps they were not born with in their personal lives.

5   An intense level of enquiry and debate about objectives and goals that dispels the status quo and keeps the process of reinvention moving ahead of the industry. The firm is not shy of constructive dissent. It fosters competitive internal trading of ideas.

6   An essentially optimistic view of the world. The firm provides a positive set of aspirations about the collective future for everyone involved. It confirms at every turn that the future is worth fighting for and that the fight will be rewarded.

7   An aura of unquantifiableness which means that the firm is perceived as more than a producer of a good or service. Its *raison d'être* is higher. The best people aspire to be part of the club.

These societal principles are collectively the fundamental source of competitive advantage for any society, whether in the business of politics, preaching or selling car tyres. Historically, they have been derived from some external authority, whether religion, family or government. But, right now, there is no credible external authority whose position remains unchallenged. Every social institution has serious question-marks hanging over it. That does not invalidate the lessons these institutions can offer. But it does open the opportunity for the corporation to pick up the mantle. Becoming a competitive society is a more sure indicator of future success than a track record of hitting EPS targets six times in a row.

Why societies fail

Most groups of human beings, whether religious houses, Nation States or corporations, fail to deliver on one or all of these seven basic counts. It is their failure to respond to these seminal needs that appears to undermine their success as organisations. All such social structures appear to crumble on a mixture of the same grounds:

1. Authority tends to become personalised, vested in the hierarchy, 'hereditary', or defined by individuals anxious to retain power. Authority which is personalised and not institutionalised as a moral framework serves short-term ambitions. It is neither likely to meet the needs of the individuals in that society nor has much chance of lasting. An individual might carry a large group of people with them for a while by force of personality. But when they finally succumb, so will the order with them. Doesn't this sound a familiar situation? From Lord Saatchi at the eponymous agency to Harold Geneen at ITT, from Margaret Thatcher's brand of conservatism to Franco's flavour of dictatorship, the same pattern is repeated. The decline of Zimbabwe in the jealous grip of Robert Mugabe is a saddening example of the damage that can be wrought by intense individualism. It is often partially for this reason that most corporations decline within a single human lifetime. It is all about the CEO, not the society of the company. Shareholders may applaud for a while but then they run for the exit before the final act. The dynastic business is an old-fashioned business.

2. The organisation fragments into splinter groups of intense self-interest. The framework holding them together is overpowered by the impetus towards individual autonomy, towards individual recognition. Groups of individuals break away to start their own endeavours. Through a process of attrition the old core withers.

In the case of the Nation State, the process of devolution has in many instances been a manageable one, with a balanced sharing of responsibility between the national centre and the local constituency. In the case of many developing countries, the individualistic political impulse has been utterly destructive. The economic decline of francophone Quebec would have saddened even Robespierre. In the case of the great religions, whilst this same process has happened, the splinter groups have tended to retain a strong blueprint of their original. Protestantism, which has fractured into innumerable groups in the US, for example, still collectively appears to retain a uniform creed.

The same is not true of companies. The parts typically become predators of their progenitor. Lucent turns on AT&T, Microsoft on IBM, Accenture on Arthur Andersen. The intense focus on individualism is totally compelling. Once unleashed it is almost irreversible. In today's business world it is endemic. But it is not the way to build a powerful entity founded on a cohesive society. It is a way to reward high-profile entrepreneurs at the expense of long-term investors.

3. Rituals become mechanical. The purpose behind them is lost and they no longer carry meaning. They are obeyed as an extension of a set of orders, unthinkingly. Any ritual that is meaningless will ultimately die, like an unused limb, and fall away into irrelevance. It will not act to hold a group of people together. It will also be subject to misappropriation by leaders or managers defending their own interests. Nothing can be more absurdly tragic than the stylised march-pasts of Kim Sung's North Korea. Symbols will, in such an environment, be deployed tactically through identity programmes, to further the self-aggrandising plans of a senior management

group anxious to stamp their mark. They become logos –
almost like personal cartouches; 'So and so is in charge and
don't forget it!' Just as the Generals running their Banana
Republics in the 1970s recast every national uniform with
each change of office, so short-term management tends to
change the corporate literature and signage to endorse their
strategy.

4. Tradition is used to buttress the status quo against the
threats posed by change. As such it relentlessly loses relevance and drags the organisation down. The ability to bring
in fresh blood dries up, the ability to grow quality people
deteriorates. With the stifling dominance of the old guard,
the prospect of change grows ever more remote. Tradition
becomes static and ossified to the point of being unintelligible to the majority of participants. The only way the chains
are broken is through eventual crisis, chronic angina, before
open-heart surgery is finally administered. These are the
symptoms most habitually associated with corporate death.
They are also the precursor to social revolution, from 1775
America to 1789 France. A static model will be broken by
the forces of inertia. The human mind is geared to breaking
chains, but broken chains mean the bad stuff has already
happened!

5. Genuine enquiry deteriorates into bureaucratic hair-
splitting, so that the important questions are skirted and the
status quo fundamentally unquestioned. Memos go out and
endless debate is stimulated about trivial questions. There is
an obsession with the details of propriety and form. Such
sclerosis led to the conquest of Christendom by Islam in
AD 500. It led to the collapse of Barings at the hands of a
rogue trader. The big, seminal issues go unanswered. No-one

is allowed to pose the big, troubling questions. The organisation becomes myopic, introverted and ultimately blind. Democracy gives way to autocracy and, with the loss of voice, commitment goes with it. Tax without representation has been shown conclusively not to work.

Most Nation States are much more tolerant of debate than companies. One important reason is that most states accommodate a Babel of different ethnicities. India alone has over a thousand dialects and, although 80 per cent are Hindu, Indian society is riddled with class distinctions. It has been periodically wracked by regional conflicts and separatist movements, but ultimately proved able to absorb these differences. The average corporation is much more homogeneous, stifled and fissile. The board is comprised of nationals. Foreign proposals are intrinsically regarded with suspicion. Dissident voices are shunned as 'off strategy'. Management only answers tough questions using the glossy medium of Microsoft Powerpoint.

6. A positive sense of purpose, of mission, is lost and replaced with rumours and speculation. The sense of forward motion is stalled. The focus is on averting the risk of any fundamental, unsettling change. Change is defined by a set of possible negative outcomes. The top dogs are firmly out to save their own skins, whatever the costs. For the rest, the most positive outcome is no outcome. Change is seen as scary. People prefer to defend what they have than seize any opportunity. The organisation becomes sclerotic. Familiar national principles and approaches are clung to like life rafts in a stormy sea. The walls go up, protectionism kicks in and industry withers in isolation from the oxygen of external ideas. The neurosis of protectionism becomes a self-reinforcing downward spiral, as the Third World development programmes of the 1970s amply demonstrated. To build you first have to break. To break you have to throw stones. The stock-market should not be mistaken for a glasshouse, but it often is by management keen to paper cracks.

7. The fallibilities and failings of the organisation are transparent to all but those inside who refuse to wake up and smell the coffee. The aura it once had is faded. The characters on whom it was founded are exposed as less than wholesome. The best graduates hold no illusion about the firm. The analysts have crawled all over it, along with the investment bankers and consultants. It is rich pickings for advisors. There is no mystery at all – no allure. It is just another national business. No-one is prepared to look ten years out because there is nothing that can possibly surprise one.

Putting the vision to work

Do any of these situations sound familiar? Most firms that perform indifferently, decline or are subject to take-over will tend to have some clear market deficiencies. Their products might be tarnished, their unit costs high, their share of voice poor, their financials flagging. But these are all symptoms, not causes. Most analysts and, indeed, most managers focus on symptoms – they are tangible, measurable and discrete. Causes are always much tougher to identify. They are systemic, intangible and complex. But at heart they usually come down to the same seven core deficiencies. It is the ability of the firm to achieve and instil a powerful, cohesive society of smart people that will determine its fate. That ability appears to rest on its mastery of that core set of social drivers. The trick we shall explore in the second half of this book is how to graft them globally into the heartland of the firm.

Like all things, organisations, whether religious or demotic, go through cycles of decay and renewal. The average Nation State, no less than corporations, has gone through long cycles – a process of stultification which precipitates revolution, and then back again. In the case of religion, the reaction of Buddha to the decadence of Hinduism, or the Protestantism of Martin Luther in the face of the rigid anachronism of German Catholicism, were all twists in long-term organic cycles. In the case of the Nation State, the great social upheavals of the Enlightenment, from Robespierre to Washington, were all responses to centuries of dynastic ossification. In each case the restoration of a viable society appears to have turned on the re-establishment of the same fundamental characteristics we have discussed. It is on these that institutional renewal appears to pivot. The corporation is on the declining part of its cycle. The objective should be to shift that position dramatically.

At its core, this is about putting people first. If there is one message that has circulated the globe and permeated every consulting report written for the past five years it is that investment in human capital yields the surest returns. Mao tried to buck this rule when he turned students into pig farmers, only to watch China being overtaken as a host for FDI by comparative dwarf states such as South Korea and Hong Kong. Those parts of the world that have continued to exclude half their talent from the workplace – their women – have lagged dramatically behind the pack. The pattern is clear – creating competitive societies is what matters, not creating competitive cash-management protocols or slick control systems. Only not many firms have twigged it!

The first half of this book has hopefully prepared the philosophical ground and demonstrated that the Nation State is a good benchmark. Now the challenge is doing something about it. That's where we go next.

7

The moral foundation: answering the great 'why?'

The purpose of modern business is simple and single-minded. Our age has made the pursuit of immediate wealth-maximisation its idol. This has made the corporation a social lynchpin, but it has also bridled the corporation inflexibly to the ethic of shareholder wealth at the expense of all other measures. The sole purpose of the modern business is to maximise immediately measurable shareholder wealth. This ethic emanates from the boardroom on down. The performance of the CEO is measured on total shareholder returns. Indeed, his stock options alone ensure that is the focus of his energy. It has taken time, but the same stimulus has now percolated through the entire organisation. If the share price takes a hammering or earnings falter, even for a quarter, then everyone knows what will happen – headcount reduction. Business is run on a quarterly basis in the knowledge that the relevant span of corporate life is three months – the same as the fruit fly!

The main tool linking the boardroom and the boiler room is the share option. Stock option plans now run deep into the muscle of most companies rather than float in the sub-cutaneous fat as they did a decade ago. This has been a fundamental underpinning of the gradual process of aligning employees and firm. But it has inevitably further exaggerated the significance of quarterly earnings. Even well-run firms make themselves martyr to quarterly budgeting and report-ing cycles above all other considerations. The paranoia is ingrained and systemic.

The ultimate goal of shareholder enrichment is indu-bitably appropriate. And wider-based ownership is a good thing. But the strategy of shareholder-return maximisation on a quarterly basis is not the same thing as building an enduring performer. On the staying-power stakes most firms are far less decisive and far less successful. Of the original constituents of the Dow, only GE is still a participant. Only 20 per cent of the FTSE 100 were there a decade ago. The pursuit of short-term, quarterly success is not a harbinger of long-term shareholder returns. We should recall that the value of a busi-ness is pretty much a reflection of its discounted future cash flows. In the long term, the long term wins out. It's the old tortoise and hare tale all over again.

How genuinely stimulated are mid-tier managers by hitting quarterly earnings targets, year in year out? Maybe for a while with the novelty of options, but thereafter? How energised can an organisation be by analysts' forecasts? The surge in employee and managerial churn over the past ten years suggests not very. The boardroom tends to assume it can project its own preoccupations on to the entire company. That is a mistake.

The moral and intellectual failure of Marxism has left us with no alternative to heroic materialism. But that isn't enough. There is no centre. The intelligent person has to ask themselves, why am I doing this? Why should I commit my energies to it? What at the end of the day will my working life have added up to? Finding no answer, cynicism inevitably fills the void. Employee churn grows. The firm falters. Options go underwater. The good people leave. It is a cycle of diminution now being experienced by the Dotcoms who once rode on an ether of miraculous quarterly revenue expectations. For any entity comprised of talented people to thrive, there has to be a higher purpose, a social aspiration that instils pride, a sense of self-worth that drives long-term value creation. This we call the firm's moral purpose.

The successful company has to have a very different conception of purpose in which, like any organism, it seeks to extend and propagate itself. As we shall describe, the firm's moral framework should shape those characteristics it legitimately aims to propagate – what the community of the firm believes in and those qualities that constitute its essential character.

Finding moral purpose

So how do we define moral purpose in any society, whether a corporation or a country? How can pursuit of moral purpose really shape a successful organisation? Let's return to our two institutional models – the state and religion.

Before the Renaissance, as the world struggled from the depths of the Dark Ages to the glories of high Gothic, morality was wedded firmly to a code of absolute rights and wrongs. This code of morality was deified into inviolability by the irrefutable force of God. Authority was external and absolute. The ultimate punishment was divine. Men owed absolute obedience to absolute rule. This pattern of psychological genuflection made it relatively simple for powerful men of the day to assume absolute moral positions, supported by reference to external authority. There was no learning, no flexibility, no room for debate. An eye for an eye.

This absolutism was only leavened for a brief period by the advent of the Renaissance, the first real breath of humanism in the evolution of civilisation up to the fourteenth century. Suddenly, the sense emerged that it was man, and man's relationship with man, that was important. The concept of morality defined by an external authority was moderated by the idea that morality was not only a matter of man's relationship with higher forces, but of man's relationship with man. Morality described how we dealt with each other, not only how we dealt with God.

It took another half a millennium for the concept of morality as a social protocol to assume permanent prominence over morality as obedience to ordained external forces. It wasn't until the 1850s that the concept of kindness and mutual support to fellow man was first properly articulated as a social obligation by the likes of James Watt and Cole Tyler. It was a self-enlightened step born of the birth of Reason and John Locke's style of liberal humanism.

The democratic principle had been established over fifty years earlier through revolution, but only now did the notion really take root that great men were appointed to help their fellow man. The dominant thrust of modern morality was born – behave morally to fellow man, and obey laws that safeguard individual rights. Laws no longer existed in an absolute divine sense, 'Thou shalt . . .'. They were created, refined and conditioned through experience and enshrined in the democratic process. The moral imperative was to safeguard constructive relationships between people. The new-found moral purpose was fundamentally a social one. Acting 'morally' became essentially an endorsement of one's legitimate claim to participation in a community.

The idea has not really evolved any further since. Now that the Wild West is long gone, no individual operates according to a personal moral code. We do not define what is right and wrong alone unless we are self-deluding or a tyrant! Morality is defined by the social group we are linked to. It underpins any society, delineating between good and bad. The moral purpose of the modern Nation State is to secure a harmonious society which grants its citizens a good standard of living. It has proved an extremely potent force precisely because it puts people's needs first and places the moral imperative at its core.

If one strips away their political appropriations and focuses on pure philosophy, the great religions place precisely the same emphasis on the place of the moral code in conditioning relationships, both with others and with ourselves. All the religions promulgate a view of what constitutes good morality. The attitude they take to moral authority is that we each have to be shown the path to self-betterment. It is the duty of religions to illuminate the path, to furnish a framework through which the individual can progress to fulfilment of their potential for good. Having identified the obstacles in our path, they all provide a framework, a methodology for redemption. The process of working through the framework, following the path, constitutes the internalisation of a moral code – a self-training course administered along closely defined lines. Like any professional environment, religion provides a ladder for emotional and spiritual fulfilment, a means to achieve moral endorsement – a fundamental need for any self-respecting person.

Hinduism, perhaps the most familiar of the exotic religions to us children of the 1960s, promulgates four paths of redemption – the reflective path through knowledge or Juana Yoga; the path that guides through love or Bhakti Yoga; the path marked out by work or Karma Yoga; and lastly the experimental path, Raja Yoga. Not so dissimilarly, Buddhism, the Puritan reaction to a decadent Hinduism of the fourth century AD, promulgates a model of redemption from the strangulating hernia of the ego and separateness through the Eightfold Path – right views; right intent; right speech; right conduct; right livelihood; right effort; right mindfulness; and right concentration. Buddhism recognises the danger run by most people of mistaking life's means, the daily process of earning a crust, as life's end. The Eightfold Path is its framework for delivery from this fate, providing a means to avoid slipping into the mire of endless self-preoccupation.

Confucianism is far less esoteric and far more readibly identifiable with the condition of the working life. It focuses on the cultivation of the social self. Its framework of self-betterment is best termed 'patterns of prestige', comprising 'Jen' or human heartedness; 'Chun Tzu' or the perfect hostess; 'Li' or savoir faire; and 'Te', the spontaneous consent that comes from good leadership. It bases its approach on the conviction that it is the inculcation of harmonious social relationships that drives the success of a people.

Islam, like Confucianism, is perhaps less accommodating of duality and alternatives than Hinduism and Buddhism. Its moral framework is more prescriptive, focused on following the straight path. There are no viable alternative routes. The 'Five Pillars' govern the private life of Muslims in their dealings with God. Both Judaism and Christianity share an almost equally unequivocal moral framework for guiding people to self-betterment – the Ten Commandments. But at heart it comes down to the same thing – moral purpose requires a means of self-redemption. That redemption is to be achieved through one's relationship with God and society at large. It cannot be accomplished in isolation. Meaning is a social construct.

In the dark jungle

Most firms have little concept of their moral purpose. The mission statement of most firms is usually a waffling piece of vacuity if ever there was one. Some adopt a veneer of objectives beyond quarterly earnings but invariably as part of the PR spin. If asked, what does it mean to be moral, few management teams would have a good answer. If asked, what is the purpose of this company doing what it does, the answer will usually be equally unclear. What you might get back is a printed statement of the firm's values, often the wooden by-product of an identity programme.

All the talk in the self-reforming corporation is about values. The ease of values statements is that they have the clarity of external rules. They are divine, absolute. The evolution of morality in advanced national societies has been from absolutism to relativism; from divine to human. As we have explored in the course of this discussion, in so many ways the modern corporation is at much the same point of development as the pre-modern state. Morality is not static. It is about interaction. A moral framework guides employees' interaction with each other. It is not about compelling individuals to adhere to a list of values. The moral framework has at its core the belief that corporations are bundles of relationships. A moral corporation guides these relationships productively.

So what is the moral function of the firm? The most moral function of the firm is to provide employment or, more specifically, to employ as many people as it can productively do so on sound employment terms. If back in the 1960s, the golden years for Western economies, you had asked a CEO how big his company was, he would probably have quantified it in terms of employees. Ten years ago, during the explosive rise of the Japanese, he would probably have defined it in terms of revenue. Now he would almost certainly talk in terms of market capitalisation. Things have not got worse. For shareholders they have got better. But what is interesting is that such terms evolve mutually exclusively. There is no comfortable trade-off. The rise of the denominator of shareholder value has been coupled with an emphasis on downsizing and reduction of the fixed employee base.

But things have also moved on in terms of our understanding of the sources of competitive advantage. The intellectual component of most goods and services is increasing rapidly, as is their service element. The limiting factor in such an environment is talent. It is not capital. The absolute number of talented people a business can attract and productively deploy will drive its competitiveness. Headcount matters. Too little of it and your rate of profits growth will be stifled. So too will your ability to differentiate and hence your sustainable margins. Most firms do not view employment as an objective. They are still caught in the factors-of-production mindset. Headcount is a cost, not an engine of output. The terms of business measurement reflect exactly that state of mind.

Being happy

Having got them in, the best litmus test of the productive capability of people is whether they are happy. The pursuit of happiness is the most fundamental moral aim – it was even enshrined by Jefferson in the Declaration of Independence. Achieving full employment and instilling happiness in the organisation is the surest route to maximising output.

We tend to assume that professional happiness is bound up solely with individual achievement. Our media place the spotlight on the individual. Reward systems are usually geared to individual performance. We live in an intensely individualised age. But assuming that is the end of the story would be a simplification. Happiness is entirely about relationships. Happiness is the by-product of recognition and acknowledgement by others. Forced into competitive isolation we quickly lose any sense of purpose. We cannot keep our own score-card with no reference to anyone else. All games, including the great game of making money, are social events. Man is a game player and he is quickly bored by Solitaire.

The issue is what creates a community of happy relationships? It cannot be achieved through aggressive pay schemes. Nor can it be achieved through excruciatingly prepared schedules of values. The moral corporation is not the one with the best-articulated values. It is the one with the best-functioning relationships. The moral corporation puts relationships first. Competitiveness is about social functionality.

Fostering a relationship community implies a set of characteristics with which most firms are intensely uncomfortable – openness of expression, dissent, dialogue, contrariety. Perhaps the single word that most fully encapsulates the sentiment is 'democracy' – the right to self-expression and enfranchised participation. In short, the right to a voice. This of course implies a serious shift in the dominant management approach of most firms. Democracy has emerged as the most stable and widespread form of social management because it is founded on a general moral purpose – the pursuit of happiness for the majority. As we shall define it more precisely, a moral framework is one that supports a democratic process of self-betterment.

Moral knowledge

Most uncomfortable of all is the fact that, for a firm to have a strong moral framework, people are required to have sufficient information to make judgements for themselves about the firm they work for. Plato's conception of the moral society was underpinned by knowledge. Unless people are given the knowledge to judge, then they cannot behave morally or better themselves. Knowledge and information are also the underpinnings of democracy. Unless they have a reasonable degree of knowledge people cannot participate in the policy debate.

Moral relationships in the workplace pivot on transfer of learning and tutelage. In the great Socratic tradition, the most moral relationship is that between pupil and master, coach and coached. Equipping people with the knowledge to participate can only be achieved through an emphasis on internal learning and tutelage. No process is more fundamentally rewarding than learning. It is also relatively cheap. It should be no surprise that the great democracies have, more than anything else, placed education at the centre of their composition. Jefferson left instructions for his tomb to be inscribed with the following sentiment, 'Here was buried

Thomas Jefferson, author of the Declaration of American Independence, of the Statute of Virginia for Religious Freedom, and father of the University of Virginia.' There was nothing about being President, nothing about the Louisiana purchase. Learning was at the forefront of his conception of democracy. As Tony Blair pronounced histrionically at his inauguration when asked about his political priorities, 'Education, education, education . . .'.

Moral management

The effect of giving people sufficient information to judge radically adjusts the management scales. We are so used to talking in terms of managers and managed as a sort of fundamental dialectic. Democratic systems are systems precisely because the distinction is blurred. Democratic systems are self-governing. Most firms are only partially self-governing. They respond to the exigencies of a predominantly external constituency – shareholders. They also shape their strategies based on the competitive pressures of the market-place. They are reflective, derivative, not self-determining. The shape they take is driven by these external forces. If the share price dives, costs are cut. If a rival innovates, they trim back the old models.

In essence, this pattern of behaviour mirrors in many ways the Nation State of the nineteenth century, conditioned by external rivalry and managed to the behest of an elite that stood outside day-to-day reality. Change is inspired from outside and management by an elite becomes an exercise in responsiveness and self-preservation. The democratic institution by comparison is much more intrinsically self-correcting. It ensures continual debate and hence change from within.

It is therefore likely to pre-empt serious externally prompted change. Governance has developed from an extrinsic to an intrinsic foundation. Morality has evolved from obedience to a supernal godly force to respect of the essential qualities that make us civilised human beings. The evolution of the political system to support the moral framework has occurred in parallel. The moral corporation is one that is continually finding its own balance. It is not strait-jacketed by the regime of corporate rules in a conventional sense, but shaped by internal, fluid, self-correcting forces.

Of course, such a proposition represents a serious threat to the currently unchallenged role of the board of directors. The principle is simple – governance cannot be without consultation. This makes the moral corporation one that incorporates a structured political process. Politics carries real stigma in the workplace. But politics is how complex relationships function within large groups of people. Politics is to the group what air is to the individual. Without it death swiftly follows!

To be effective, a moral framework cannot simply be a method of control – it cannot be the same as a list of values or a mission statement. The concept of 'values' is comfortable to managers because they are susceptible to the orderliness of strategy. For the same reason they are intensely limiting. As with the great religions, a moral framework also has to be a framework for personal redemption. It is something that guides behaviour through managing aspirations. Unless it holds the prospect of self-betterment, both moral and material, then it can never stimulate. A moral framework motivates by driving a process of education, of acquisition of skills that will better the employee's ability to contribute to the community and thereby win social endorsement. The end is moral because it is the fulfilment of a valued societal role. The end is also moral because it results in self-betterment and happiness. That also, by the way, makes good returns!

Finding the heartland of the firm

Firms that are highly differentiated as communities tend to have a clear sense of what they stand for, which in turn conditions the nature of the product or service they deliver. Their sense of fulfilment stems from a strong conviction that their approach to satisfying customers is morally laudable. They feel good about what they do. Work is a personal and collective moral fulfilment. They have a missionary zeal to enlighten as many people and markets as they possibly can. Once a firm is set on such a cause, a cause for the right of the customer and employee, then it gathers its own momentum. The moral objective is the one that fundamentally matters to people.

We can say something clear about the characteristics of a moral corporation. It is likely to focus its efforts not on measuring individual effort but on optmising the relationships between people. It is likely to emphasise maximising the number of talented individuals it is prepared to support in its community. It will tend to place a high degree of importance on securing their happiness and furthering their ability to improve their lot. It will not be heavy-handed in promulgating values. It will view itself as a place of learning and self-improvement. The dissemination of ideas and information will be a sine qua non. Above all, it will be grounded in a political process rather than a corporate strategy, which allows voices to be heard. The dominant characteristic of the moral framework of the firm is that it is motivational, not regulatory.

It defines our aspirations; it prescribes what makes us admired by our peers; it isolates those things we strive to achieve. It works through us.

The moral objective is to increase people's happiness, both employees and customers. That doesn't sound very strategic! But, after all, strategy does not actually work very well in people businesses. Countries do not have strategies. Societies do not have strategies. Strategy is a term co-opted from the battlefield. In the Klauswitzian schema protagonists are divided and marshalled for a single violent event. Discipline matters more than individual innovation. Decisions come solely from the top. Firms or any other sorts of social construct are, of course, very different. The process gluing people into order is not marshalling. But they do have to be governed. This governance process is called politics. A political system has leadership but the system is greater and more enduring than the leader.

What governance structure is necessary to support such a system? There are clear limitations to the current system of the board. It is often dominated absolutely by the CEO or Chairman. Its principal role is serving as an externally facing body for the investor community. The mediators are the non-executive directors who are meant to show dispassion and disinterest but who, in reality, have little clout and are usually concerned to preserve their stipends. It is a small body typically remote from the coal-face whose workings are opaque. No-one sees the minutes. The doors are closed. Most mid-tier managers will not even meet the members, let alone be privy to their thought-processes.

The real weakness of this system is that it is not attuned to supporting a moral framework such as we have described, nor to supporting the other elements of social competitiveness we shall work through. But what structure can viably replace it? It is tempting to propose that the national political process would constitute a viable model – of two legislative houses, each balancing the other. But this is not realistic given the overriding fiduciary responsibility of boards to their shareholders and creditors. The concept of the board is hard to replace viably for all its weaknesses.

The real governance issue is the composition of the board, its proximity to the business and its responsiveness to its internal constituencies. Boards on the whole need to be enriched so that their investor focus is balanced by an internal-management focus which reflects the need to inject and articulate a sense of purpose. Democratising the voice of the firm means including a cross-section of individuals drawn from all areas. Most boards are comparatively small – say 15 for a corporation of 15 000. There is ample scope for enlarging them whilst still preserving a core executive. If non-execs traditionally provide an outside perspective, internal non-execs should provide an internal perspective so often lacking. This cross-section should run deep through the core of the company.

The fiduciary board also needs to be fed by sub-boards with an exclusively operating focus and a mandate to discuss and debate key issues of operations and strategy – forums of debate with the power to influence management decisions and which then pass recommendations up to the board for review, much as motions are tabled in Parliament or Congress. The appointment process to these boards is also critical. Board accountability means insider non-execs must effectively be voted in on a rotating basis from within the organisation. It means that a truly capable person who thoroughly embodies the virtues espoused by the firm should aspire to participate at the top. There can be no glass ceiling.

The issue of accountability also has to extend to the board in totality. The moment of accountability for most boards is the Annual General Meeting of shareholders and, ancillary to that, the quarterly analysts' presentations. Bizarrely, these have no counterpart internally. There is no internal AGM where employees get the opportunity to ask the tough questions. There are no quarterly reviews where performance is explained. That fact is at the heart of the absolute shareholder bias of most firms. Unfortunately, there are few if any models of balanced governance. The German model of the Advisory Board and *Werkscouncil* reflects aspects of what we have proposed, but associated unionisation has paralysed the development of many *Mittelstand*.

What we have described has more the appearance of a political construct than a conventional board. But what it does not obviate is the need for the setting of moral goals. There is a lot of literature on corporate morality. It mostly focuses on corporate responsibility – what the firm owes in fealty to the communities in which it operates. The average corporation endows around 0.2 per cent of its pre-tax profits to good causes. At the philanthropic extreme, some firms have established foundations of immense economic weight. The Wellcome Trust provides 40 per cent of all cash dedicated to primary research in the UK. The great patrons of Renaissance Florence were the obscenely wealthy traders.

This is of course very laudable, and many great cultural institutions would wither without it – from opera to Renoir. But it is not the foundation of morality in the corporation. It is a sort of tokenism, a giving of alms – essential, useful, but not an expression of fundamental morality on part of the giver. It is also often self-promoting, run by the marketing department to buy share of consciousness rather than conscience. Firms should not mistake having a conscience with having a moral objective. Once an organisation finds its sense of moral purpose it is unstoppable.

8

The selfish gene: learning to think 'us', not 'me, me, me . . .'

There is a brazen paradox at the heart of the global village. Culture and taste are converging in a way they have not done since the Roman Empire. Tourism is growing at 9 per cent a year and now ranks as one of the world's largest industries. There are tens of millions of teenagers who, having been raised on a multimedia-rich diet, have a lot more in common with each other than with older members of their own culture. Cultures are, on the face of it, converging at tremendous speed.

But there is the equally strong counter-force at play of fragmentation. The fifty or so years since the Second World War have emerged as the era of the individual. Family units have eroded dramatically, along with the other foundations of community, from churches to Boy Scouts brigades. The emphasis on individual competition has never been greater. We compete alone for selfish rewards. Combine that with the ascendancy of psychoanalysis – the conviction that we each alone have to grasp our mental flaws and repair them – and what should be convergence is in fact atomisation. We are all locked in a cell of self, each feeding our own dreams of conquest. We might all consume in a similar manner but we do so alone.

The impact on the child of the fifties, sixties and seventies is ambivalent. The breaking of ties of allegiance has meant more freedom of expression, greater ambition, and more opportunity for personal wealth creation. Art has been democratised and, with it, the leisure time to enjoy it. But the downsides of extreme competitive isolation are also coming into sharper focus. The walls of the cell of self impose an intense psychological strain on us all.

How has this sea change affected the company? To a large degree it has been positive. All social institutions need shaking up now and then. Personal productivity and creativity have increased along with the common appetite to create wealth. But, as the cycle has gone another turn, it has also driven the difficulty most firms are experiencing in trying to differentiate. Employee churn has increased dramatically, disaffection has never been higher, the identification between employee and firm is at a historical nadir. Socially most firms are enfeebled. The lack of cohesion is amply demonstrated by the ready defection of senior corporate staff to the illusion briefly offered by Dotcoms in mid-1999. Any scent of something better and they are gone. It is clear that the average firm gives little attention to inculcating a sense of wholehearted participation by its employee-base in the future of the organisation. There is no confidence amongst top management that it would be in their interests to do so.

There is probably little confidence they will even be around in the future to care. The interests of the firm and those of its employees remain distinct. If the firm has a quarterly horizon, the average talented employee probably has no more than an annual one.

The heave of humanism

Up until 1850, the Nation State also failed to evolve a powerful framework for linking individual and collective interests. The national purpose was essentially an elitist game of chess played out by a tiny, inbred minority, largely for the benefit of themselves and their coterie – the court. Rules were absolute and quixotic. Punishments were extreme, choice unheard of, kindness a whim and subservient to the realpolitik of international conflict. The monarchical system provided cohesion, but this was based on moral coercion and absolutism. The elitist dictatorship survived as the dominant political form up until the 1970s with the ousting of Salazar and the death of Franco. It was only after 1973 that the liberal democracy gained unrivalled dominance. The essential underpinnings of that change had been laid a hundred and fifty years before by the humanists – the acknowledgement that man mattered more than the divine system.

Perhaps the only Western institution to have countered the political thrust of the times was the Church. It emerged into real prominence after 1100. One of its key strengths was that it was basically a democratic institution where pure ability made its way. Men of intelligence normally took holy orders and could rise from obscurity to positions of immense influence, from Wolsey to Pope Innocent IX. Another of its enormous strengths was its internationalism. It owed no geographical allegiance. The great churchmen of the eleventh and twelfth centuries came from all over Europe. Perhaps the greatest mind of the day, Anselm, came from obscure Aosta to become Archbishop of Canterbury. These men identified more closely with the community of the Church than with their state. Not coincidentally, nearly all the steps upwards in civilisation have been made in such circumstances of internationalism.

There were other 'epiphanies' in the darkness of those middle centuries. That great heave of social creativity – the Renaissance – was of course founded on humanism. The patriarchs of Florence and Siena believed firmly, as did the Greek philosopher Protagoras, that 'Man is the measure of all things.' From Salutati onwards, the Florentine chancellors were scholars who believed that learning could be used to achieve a happier life. They were believers in the application of free intelligence to public affairs. Chancellors such as Leonardo Bruni saw the Florentine Republic as reviving the virtues of Greece and Rome. Humanity and its achievements were to be gloried in. The ultimate reward for the outstanding individual was fame.

This was all in intense contrast to the medieval view of man's inadequacies in the face of God. The architecture of Florence assumed a more human scale. The buildings were an assertion of the dignity of man, not a celebration of inexorable divine forces. One of the great military leaders of the Florentine Republic, the first Duke of Urbino, observed that the quality most necessary for ruling a kingdom was 'essere umano' – to be human. That is a far cry from virtually every ruler before or since, from Henry V to Queen Victoria.

The flame occasionally and briefly burst back into life. The same spirit of humanism illuminated and electrified the society of Amsterdam in the 1450s. The spirit even spilled over into that isolated island, Britain. Sir Thomas More, friend of the reforming humanist Erasmus, penned *Utopia* in the glow of that same fervour. But it was not until the 1850s that the political system of the state began to aspire to that condition consciously, of guarding individual rights and achieving a general state of contentedness.

The first discovery and exploitation of the means for mechanical production coincided with the first organised attempts to improve the general human lot. The first large iron foundries, like the Carron Works or Coalbrookdale, burst upon the unsuspecting rural world at about the same time that Sir Frederick Eden published the first ever sociological survey, *The State of the Poor*. Howard's book on penal reform was published in 1777 and Clarkson's essay on slavery in 1785. By 1800 the concept of kindness and benevolence firmly entered the intellectual consciousness. The idea that the moral function of society was to better the lot of the majority assumed its rightful place.

It had taken a thousand years for the Nation State to crystallise a sense of purpose which that other great institution, religion, had been propounding from the outset. The backdrop to political developments over that thousand-year period was the constant refrain sustained by the Church. All the great religions placed equal importance on moving beyond personal concerns and an egocentric view of progress towards a collective, 'de-personalised' view of the world. Obsessive personalisation was seen as intensely limiting to development. It was also seen as corrosive to personal well-being. Success was to be achieved with others and through others. The religions all lament the pitfalls of competitive isolation that ultimately force man into conflict both with himself and with others. Religion in general focuses on this issue of at-one-ness, re-binding, or, in its Greek root, *re-ligio*. It is an essentially humanist impulse, the objective of which is happiness.

Probably at one end of the spectrum on the anti-ego trail is Hinduism. Hinduism regards the centring of meaning on the self as far too limiting. As a religion it is preoccupied with the search for the larger whole to relieve life of its triviality. Religion becomes a quest for meaning beyond self-centredness. The same theme of release is echoed in the other great religions. In Christianity the release from the confines of the ego is achieved via love – love for one's fellow men and women. Central to the concept of union, the opposite of separateness, is the idea of surrender – surrender to greater goals than those achievable by personal, muscular, egotistical exertion. As William James put it, 'In those states of mind which fall short of religion, surrender is submitted to as an imposition of necessity and the sacrifice is undergone at the very best without complaint. In the religious life, on the contrary, surrender and sacrifice are positively espoused.'[2] The philosophical foundation of the quest for a better state of being was clearly laid down.

Buying civilisation

Of course, the progress from rival dynasties to mature democracies was not simply the product of philosophical shifts. It was underpinned by the gradual development of some fundamental tools of social management – most importantly, an impartial process of law, and a systematic protocol for raising

---

[2] See James, William. *The Varieties of Religious Experience*. Macmillan, 1961.

revenue to finance collective services – the much maligned institution of taxation.

The underpinning of the movement towards humanism was progress from the capricious dictates of an elite to a set of rules of governance based on impartial premises and moral imperatives. As we have explored, the moral framework places the government of relationships at its heart. But, to be effective operationally, such mores have to be enshrined in a defensible protocol. We call that protocol the Law. All countries are founded on their judicial process. The key benefit of participating in a society is that we are given social protection by laws and therefore derive more security collectively than we could do alone. The weaker the judicial process, the weaker the society. A weak judiciary usually means it is incapable of being self-governing and will become ripe for dictatorship.

The legal system is, of course, fundamentally self-administering and independent. From its instigation with the Magna Carta, it has divorced the rights of citizens from the force of political power. It upholds moral standards that most people respect. The value system is ingrained. It also tends to be unique by territory and lends each culture something of its special cohesion. It inspires the confidence to speak out and defend one's point of view. Inalienable rights imbue a society with the confidence to create value. They cannot be subverted by political whim.

Companies are subject to the judicial process of each territory in which they operate. But, extraordinarily, they tend not have any documented system of rules to govern their own societies. In a legal sense of development, the firm resembles the eighteenth-century state. There is a contract between employer and employee which stipulates what they must do to retain their employment. But, outside these contractual parameters, the relationship is non-specific. It is also non-reciprocal. There is no framework to inspire trust in the system. The inevitable corollary is that we work for money and that's it. Compensation is everything.

In the case of national society, the law is a service we all enjoy the benefit of, even if sometimes it is hard to see it that way. But no service comes for free. We all pay for it through that institution called taxation. Paying tax is a fundamental underpinning of stakeholder society. As Lord Denning observed, 'I pay tax to buy civilisation.' Paying tax means we subscribe to the moral code and moral purpose of our society. It also means we require our view to be represented. Tax and representation are inexorably tied together. In a very real way it requires us to become shareholders, which also means we tend to care about the outcome. It should not therefore be surprising that people typically express far more passionate opinions about national issues than they do about work – the difference being that they are stakeholders in one and pay-cheque receivers in the other.

This systemic, reciprocal relationship of national society is missing in companies. The sole tax an employee gives is time in return for pay. One nascent instance of a notional tax in the corporate world is stock options in lieu of salary or bonus. The better you do the more right you have to contribute. The other, more complete, model is the professional partnership. But, as we have already discussed, the partnership model is impracticable for most firms. The fact is that the reciprocal contract between citizen and state, founded on a bedrock of law and tax, is entirely absent in the vast majority of firms.

Beyond the judiciary, one of the key applications of tax money is of course education – the underpinning of social cohesion. By learning together we also learn to live together.

Tony Blair heralded the first term labour had secured in office for 17 years with the invocation, 'Education, education, education . . .'. But on this score countries are far from being paragons of virtue. The average Nation State certainly under-invests in education. But corporations are lamentably worse. The average corporation competes based on the talents of its employees but does not reinvest in its social development. That means its social efficiency and robustness are severely undermined.

Education, unlike most reward schemes, is fundamentally social in nature. It is conducted in groups, it involves the transmission of knowledge from one generation to the next and tends to impart a similar way of thinking, a bond of commonality that lasts a lifetime. Education of course also requires much more thought than a classical reward scheme dreamt up by Towers Perrin or Hays. It presupposes a curriculum, a language, a methodology, and trained educa-tors. That poses real challenges.

The first real hurdle most firms face is unwillingness to spend cash on such an investment when the returns are not immediate and the benefit unquantifiable. Cash spent on reward systems is only spent once and only yields a one-time benefit. People quickly forget their initial euphoria at getting the bonus cheque. Cash on education, by contrast, will yield a future return. It is an investment item. Even in the shorter term there is payback. Education will pretty quickly dampen employee churn – few people leave a firm when they are learning at a steep rate – again saving budget.

Even if the budget constraint is overcome, there is one problem however – who will do the teaching? Most smart senior employees no longer see themselves as teachers – dissemination of knowledge would potentially undermine their personal equity. The firm has a serious obstacle to overcome. The willingness of firms to outsource executive education to MBA institutions has probably been the biggest surrender of core value to an external supplier of the entire core-competency movement. If education is not a core competence, the firm has little chance of sustaining any unique competence at all for very long!

It has clearly been shown that the state with the highest-educated inhabitants will be the most socially cohesive and the most competitive. It's that simple! As Confucius predicted, the one with the highest wen is the winner! But education is only a subset of a triumvirate of forces, all of which are interdependent – law, tax and education. No social contract that unites large numbers of people can work in the absence of any of them.

The accountable boss

The individualistic imperative that plagues firms often emanates from the leader – the top dog. The role of leadership in a modern social system is distinct. The emergence of the modern political system marks the movement away from the oligarch model to a governmental process with in-built accountability. Power exists through a governmental process, characterised by a system of checks and balances. In such an entity, the CEO's job is that of the leader of a fractious political party, creating coalitions to get an agenda implemented. His method has to be as consensual as the circumstances will allow.

The quality of the leadership in Nation States is not necessarily any better than that found in companies. Most political leaders suffer the same weakness as their counterparts in business. On the whole, he (it almost always is a he) is a rapacious egotist, prepared to promise what in his heart he often knows cannot be delivered, in order to get into power. The virtues of the leaders of Asian developmental states like Taiwan, who subordinate their private passion to the public interest, are rare. The beauty of the modern democracy, however, is that the leader is only a small part of a multifaceted machine. The institutionalisation of debate, combined with the balance of both opposition and legislatures, enshrines a system of checks and balances. The system itself is greater than the individual. This reduces, although not eliminates, the huge risk connected with dependency on one man's judgement – the oligarch's whim. The firm, by contrast, tends to be fully exposed.

The CEO role in most companies reflects the lack of sophistication of the internal political process, which is itself a reflection of the lack of importance attached to people. Political CEOs are no more long-lived than their corporate counterparts. The big difference is that the system to which they are appointed is much more robust and multifaceted. In the context of a democracy, their ability to make or destroy is much more limited and collective interests have to be respected. That translates directly into the social durability of the institution. The firm with a strong moral framework will be more enduring than the firm reliant on an individual.

Instead of a single star, the firm like any society should have a constellation of stars throughout the organisation, each of whom will serve as a role model for aspiring employees, or as Lao-tzu put it more eloquently, 'A leader is best when people barely know that he exists. Of a good leader who talks little, when his work is done, his aim fulfiled, they will say "we did this ourselves".'[3] The board should not be

---

[3] See Waley, Arthur. *The Way and Its Power*. Allen and Unwin, 1958.

passive. It should be comprised of a collection of outstanding individuals, each capable of running an enterprise and each sharing a passion for the firm. The fact that shareholders are prepared to risk a situation where one man carries the entire firm is extraordinary if you think about it. If, at one extreme, the CEO and CFO went down in a plane crash, how would this affect the average corporation's stock price?

The prestidigitations of the invisible hand

Of course, some people would question whether a political process of governance is relevant at all. A political process is necessary in any society, more so than individual leadership. That means government is also necessarily comprised of potentially competing constituencies. This is a profoundly unfashionable proposition. Government is widely touted to be an inefficient form of management. It absorbs a significant amount of overhead. Its decision making can be comparatively slow. It also tends to be interventionist. Ricardo and his acolytes first propounded that governments should take a back seat as redistributors in an essentially self-regulating free market for goods and services. Ever since, this has been a war cry for politicians seeking re-election through tax cuts. And it has indeed become received practice.

In reality the Ricardian global market is only an extremely recent phenomenon. It is in its infancy and effectively untested. The freeing of short-term capital flows only happened in the wake of German unity in 1990, which proclaimed the end of the government-centred design for the world created at Bretton Woods. German unity acted as a catalyst for the creation of a world labour market, catapulting three million people on to the world labour market, from the former Soviet Union, China and India. At the same time, resolution of the debt crisis under US Secretary Brady enabled mid-income debtor countries to restructure their debt through officially sponsored debt reduction programmes tied to broad policies of liberalisation, stabilisation and privatisation. It was this that spurred Mexico to negotiate the NAFTA accord and Brazil and Argentina to form Mercosur. The end of the cold war and import substitution also opened up steep cost gradients between regions, with the average labour costs of Germany two hundred times higher than those of south-east Asia. This further drove the urge to globalise production. The result was a sudden spurt of global trade. The invisible hand had got the upper hand. 'Big government' was out. At least that was the rallying cry.

But things are not so simple. The invisible hand is about as mythical as the Invisible Man. The Ricardian vision of open, consolidated markets has been balanced in equal force by the emergence of the ethnic region as a politically powerful unit, run by strong local management. The promise of the EU superstate looks almost absurd in a continent characterised by intense regionalism. North America is no better. Canada is famously now divided into four. The swath within a hundred miles of the US border looks south to NAFTA. Quebec looks east to France. Ontario is effectively part of the Midwest. The far West looks to Asia Pacific, which in turn mirrors the same tensions. In Indonesia per capita income varies by as much as a factor of six amongst its dependencies. In China the discrepancy is ten. These states are inevitably bound to pursue regional and not national development. The same is true of the mature economies of Spain, Italy and even the jolly UK. The political process is adamantly the dominant force. The question is less whether the political process is relevant, but rather what form it should take and how it should optimise its effectiveness.

The democratic endgame

The key index of the sophistication of a political process is its robustness as an impartial system of management. Social institutions, whether geopolitical units or corporations, that begin with a rigid personalised framework conceived by a founder, whether Bill Gates or Washington, will almost inevitably evolve over time to a more democratic means of self-governance. Democracy is inevitable with growth and sophistication. As a community becomes larger it is forced to decentralise management. Over time the number of significant voices grows. The complexity of development requires an adaptive strategy, a strategy that is increasingly consensus-driven.

As a system, it also becomes essentially depersonalised. Over time the institution begins to generate its own peculiar character, independent of any particular individual, although it might reflect in a number of ways the original founding spirit. Unless a collective body does broadly reflect the interests of all participants, it will ultimately fragment, and then dissolve. This is precisely what happens with the majority of corporations which have an average life span of 40 years. They fail to move beyond oligarchy to a political framework that provides a compelling collective purpose to the individuals who comprise it. Pieces break away through MBOs or the resignation of key individuals. Such firms ultimately wind up being taken over, merging or going bust. This is true of countries as much as it is of companies. Provided human beings are involved, the same social rules apply.

Finding the heartland of the firm

Humanism can readily be dismissed as namby-pamby dreaming, irrelevant to the cut-throat world of contemporary business. But espousing robust inclusiveness does not mean a loss of competitive spirit. Quite the reverse. A strong society will also be highly competitive with rival societies. That is precisely the story of the Nation State. No social entity has been more robustly competitive in the pursuit of comparative advantage. The imbalances of the world economy bear testimony to the incompatible policies pursued by states in their permanent attempt to make relative or absolute gains over competitors. There is nothing soft about thinking social.

The fact is that firms need a more coherent system to engage motivated collective energy. Movement away from the old concept of the company to what is best termed a 'commercial society' offers a positive route forward. Critical components of this are an impartial system for evaluation and judgement, an ethic that requires employees to invest in the system, and a system that places emphasis on personal formation – bettering the human assets that make up the firm. Unless firms can get this right, they will remain intensely vulnerable to knowledge migration as mere fragile clusters of migratory talent.

To date, the main thrust of firms seeking to harness collective energy has been less than effectual. The dominant 'enlightened' paradigm of the 1990s has been the 'team'. Cross-functional team structures are often the result of reengineering exercises, designed with the intention of streamlining internal transactions. The irony of teams is that, whilst they are meant to integrate across functions, they tend to lead to organisational fragmentation. Teams work optimally with no more than 14 people. If they work well, each team will tend to become quite competitive with other groups, proprietorial and defensive. In essence they will start to behave like an independent firm. As a result, the larger firm risks losing the power of its wholeness.

In reality larger companies are founded on a network of relationships, the health of which is measurable by the volume and diversity of communications. Structural solutions such as teams which cut across these networks sever the fluid medium of the network and staunch the healthy flow of information – the information that is the life-blood of any modern company. Imposing rigid structures on organic entities usually means the organism dies. The same heavy-handedness characterises the debate about remuneration strategies. There is nothing wrong with the intention. The error comes in the assumption that motivational tools need to be linked umbilically to reward schemes and cash. The social motive is the most powerful there is. It needs no excuse.

On a final note, in our web-frenzied age, large firms tend to get dismissed as dinosaurs, clumsy beasts that cannot respond to market change. But in this game of creating societies, size in fact has decisive advantages. The advantage large organisations have over small ones is, at the risk of banality, their size. Size means more ideas, more cash for ideas, better distribution, economies of scale to achieve competitive costs, greater capacity to absorb the risks associated with new products and the ability to open up new markets. Above all, size means a strong corporate personality that can stamp its mark on the hostile landscape. Larger societies almost always conquer smaller ones.

9

The identity game: answering the great 'who am I?'

Any of us over 40 periodically malign the fact that looks play an absurdly overinflated role in our modern society. Why, we ask, does everyone worship Claudia Schiffer or Iman? Surely brains and character matter more? The media and the consuming public alike are infatuated with glamour. We have been conditioned to use our visual antennae to judge everything. We have become *cognoscenti* of the language of brands.

The obsession with looks has profound limitations and also moral implications. But it is symptomatic of a deeper human condition – the hunger we all share to possess an identity which is immediately respected, admired or envied by our fellow man. Identity, and particularly visual identity, is not simply a vanity. It is a fundamentally social impulse.

We are defined by the group we belong to. The degree of affinity between the individual and the whole correlates directly to the strength of a society. Social exclusion is accompanied by a collapse of identity and self-worth. That is why banishment has been the next best punishment after death.

The Nation State only really discovered a self-conscious sense of identity about a hundred and fifty years ago. The birth of the modern Nation State was as much a marketing event as anything else. It was when it came to sell itself as a package, an attraction, that it discovered the value of having a distinct identity to set it apart. The Paris *Exposition Universelle* of 1855, the Great Exhibition of 1851 at Crystal Palace, the Philadelphia Centennial of 1876 – all were acts of conscious self-reinvention. The penning of the national anthem, the sewing of the national flag, the crowning of the Poet Laureate – all were manifestations of the urge to celebrate one's identity as a social player in a competitive world of rivals. The emergence of the modern state as a cohesive social unit was bound up with the development of a sense of identity. Without identity society does not really exist.

The modern national identity is no longer the prescriptive concept it was back in the 1850s. Countries can rather be identified with a national style that has evolved organically over time. But this style also tends to be remarkably persistent and pervasive despite the organic, chaotic nature of its evolution. In Holland it is blue-glazed Delft tiles, in Spain sangria, in England bone china and unreliable sports cars. National identity has a million small manifestations, the smallest of which clearly identifies the beast. The emergence of local regions as viable political entities has reinforced the intensity of identity, usually founded on long-standing ethnic tradition. Despite the much-vaunted Californianisation of tastes, a Catalan is proud of being a

Catalan, a Basque of being a Basque. The Welsh still say 'boyo'. The identity of regions is so powerful it even undermines the relevance of national identity. The ultimate social unit is defined by its identity and without a strong identity no social unit will endure.

For many people this means a sort of schizophrenia. Am I more Spanish or Catalan? Which identity shall I assume? Should I teach my child Gaelic as well as English? Companies are also typically schizophrenic. Corporations always carry two logos – their own and that of their home state. In light of the dominant Ricardian zeal this ambivalence has made them nervous. Their efforts to ditch their national identities and emphasise their own has led to crude oversimplification. The logo is a fundamentally limiting attempt to junk complex identity in favour of simplified branding. It is like a teenager getting a pierced tongue to divorce herself from her parents.

Symbolic man

At the heart of identity are symbols. The role of symbols is twofold – they provide meaning and they provide a common language. They are part of the glue holding societies together. A powerful symbol is easily reproducible without loss of recognition – a cross is a cross whether it is an intricate piece of silver-work or simply two wooden sticks tied together. Hence the chance of it retaining relevance across highly dispersed geographies – where there is no documentation to explain its meaning and where it may suffer minor changes in terms of stylistic representation – is all the greater. It is a universal language within the community that gave rise to it. Simply by seeing or feeling an icon a set of ideas is

passively invoked. This invocation is closely bound up with
a sense of belonging, of participation, and hence is intensely
social in nature. The stronger the delineation and the more
highly evolved its iconography, the stronger will be the
community. A community is defined by its symbols.

The apogee of the symbolic mind was probably around
1300, in the wake of the building of the great cathedrals at
Chartres and Rheims. Medieval man perceived the reliefs and
triptychs that adorned these special places as nothing less
than symbols or tokens of an ideal order which was the only
true reality. That high point of civilisation of the late Middle
Ages, the Renaissance, raised the visual symbol to its heights.
Raphael's *Galatea* and *School of Athens* emerged as paragons
of symbolism. The visual pointed the way to ultimate truths.

The birth of symbolism was not uniform across civilisations. The aggressive nomadic societies – Israel, Islam, the
Protestant north – always conceived of their gods as male.
Male religions have produced little imagery. It is the female
religions of Egypt, France, India and China, which balanced
the male with a female role in creationism, that have produced all the great symbolic art. The corporation is an
ostensibly male structure. This perhaps accounts for its lack
of understanding of the power of symbolism.

Whatever their level of comfort with symbolism, all the
great religions share fundamentally symbolic languages. Each
great religion has its text: Hinduism the Vedas; Confucianism
the Classics; Judaism the Torah; Christianity the Bible; and
Islam the Koran. As well as imparting knowledge, each text
also functions as a symbol of higher truths. At one extreme
the Koran is not even historical but directly doctrinal. It is
not about the truth; it is the truth. Symbol and symbolised
converge. But all the texts share this quality to a degree.
They are not ripping yarns. They are symbols of faith and

the qualities that faith embodies. They bind their communities together.

There is also a subtle point at which symbol and ritual merge. The great religions have taken the seminal need for identity and turned it into a set of fundamental markers governing spiritual life through from the ceremonial days that mark the calendar, each with its own processions, to the ritualised gestures and patterns of behaviour which make religious events religious. Even for relative agnostics, rituals such as Christmas, Easter or Ramadan underpin their family lives. They are ostensibly symbolic events but the ritual has taken over until they are so ingrained in our culture that the symbolism is almost forgotten.

Literate man

Everything we have described thus far is visual. But identity is not exclusively associated with visual symbols. This false assumption has been inculcated by the overwhelming dominance of branding in modern life. Even universities have become branded goods! Visual symbolism has its limitations as a social glue. The widespread transition from images to words was made by civilisation back in the 1500s for good reason. Only corporate thinking has not yet caught up in most cases!

Up until Charlemagne, few rulers were literate. Alfred the Great could read but he could never write. Charlemagne was the first great ruler to emerge from the illiterate nullity of the Dark Ages. It was through him that the Atlantic world re-established contact with the ancient culture of the Mediterranean. Seminal to the effort was literature. Our whole knowledge of ancient literature is due to collecting and copying that began under Charlemagne. In copying these manuscripts his scribes arrived at the most beautiful lettering ever invented and also the most practical. When the Renaissance humanists wanted to find a clear and elegant substitute for their crabbed gothic script they revived the Carolingian. It has survived in more or less the same form until today.

If civilisation were not to wither like the society of Egypt, it had to draw life from deeper roots than those that had nourished the intellectual triumphs of the Renaissance. Out of this sea change, marked by the Lutheran Reformation, a new civilisation was created. But it was one based on words, not images. The great images of the Middle Ages were broken up on the anvil of the Reformation. Luther translated the Bible into demotic German and so gave normal people the tools for thought. There was no going back. Man, of course, always returns to his symbols. It was this impulse that fuelled the Counter-Reformation. The Catholic revival gave ordinary people the old solace of ritual, images and symbols. But it was too late – language had already stolen the march on visual prompts as the driver of social differentiation.

Language is a more consistent and versatile medium of identity than visual symbols. It does not limit ideas, it does not prescribe expression. It simply enables a group versed in that particular language to share thoughts, feelings and concepts. The most powerful symbols are those that are fluid and adaptable but part of a consistent patina. The more coherent, the more universal a language, the more robust will be a society, tolerating both fruitful debate and fostering greater understanding. As a consequence, the more sophisticated a community's language, the more advanced will be its ideas. Also, perhaps more importantly, the more able that community will be to export its ideas and approaches to other

communities and markets. Intellectual and linguistic conquest is far more enduring than military victory. That is why
Anglicisation is almost as feared by the French establishment
as was Hitler.

Corporate illiteracy

The business world has begun more recently to awaken to the
extraordinary power of ritual and symbolism to foster a strong
collective identity. It has even spawned an industry called
Corporate Identity Design. At the conventional end, this
revolves around the creation of the ubiquitous corporate logo
and glossy, high-resolution literature. The budgets to put
these programmes in place can sometimes be truly mind-
boggling. British Telecom's facelift in the early nineties was
rumoured to have run up a bill of £150 million, AT&T's
revamp in the same period probably cost around the same,
although both firms have in the process been through
consumer-driven revolutions that, temporarily at least, trans-
formed their competitiveness.

The average corporation is once again at the stage of evolution at which the Nation State was before the Renaissance.
As in so many regards, the average firm shows itself to be a
relatively primitive form of social organisation. The corporation is not attuned to symbolism. It is attuned to brands.
Brands are the life-blood of consumerism. But over-reliance on
the process has led to a belief that the same concept is trans-
posable to complex social environments such as companies or
even countries. Most corporate identity initiatives still suffer
this limitation of a focus on branding. An employee does not
interact with their firm the same way they do with a can of
Coke! Brands work with consumers because the relationship

of the product and consumer is simple. However the ad agency planners dress it up, it is at heart a gratification/aspiration event. The relationship of employee and firm is an infinitely more complex social phenomenon.

The big difference between most corporate identity programmes and the symbolist ritual of the great religions is that between form and content. Religious symbolism serves a purpose. Like words, it is a route to a truth which is complex to explain but which can be more readily and universally accessed through symbols. The same cannot be said of many corporate identity programmes. A corporate logo does not typically give rise to a set of values. It does not invoke a code of behaviour. It simply denotes a brand. A brand is very different from an icon or symbol. It connotes certain values of consumption, of group or individual endorsement. It does not connote a set of profoundly held beliefs. The fact that an identity programme is usually a one-time discrete revamp, often contracted out to a few-person consultancy, says a lot about the degree of genuine identification between the brand identity and the company.

Firms also tend to be dogmatic and prescriptive in policing their identity programmes. Logo schemes are rarely adaptable. They will be governed by strict guidelines, specifying the font that must be used, the precise colours, the exact configuration on a page. These programmes are policed by 'logo-cops'; they are regulated for uniformity. The driving impulse is to render the vaguely chaotic, organic nature of most firms which have evolved across different countries over time, into something that is the same everywhere. It is the Coke dream.

Such rigidity is anathema to symbolism, as are the quixotic and regular revamps to which companies regularly subject their own identities. Symbolism is absorbed and evolves fluidly over time based on a core heritage. When companies merge, one identity is discarded and another adopted much like a corporate change of clothes. In 1998 in the US alone 240 major corporations changed their identities. This means annually a whole history of iconography gets swept away and with it all the meaning, heritage and values wrapped up with it.

Of course, visualisation has its role. One characteristic of countries is that they have borders and maps. The map allows the visualisation of what otherwise can be a highly subjective, ungraspable entity. People like pictures because they render abstractions concrete. Nobody can endure too much abstraction. Most employees probably have a hard time conceptualising the company for which they work. They have an even harder time conceptualising its strategy. Few firms can offer a map of their world by which employees can navigate their way around. Vasco da Gama would have been bemused!

By virtue of the ascendancy of marketing, firms have now grasped the role of visual identity. However, most senior managers have not really understood the role of language as an underpinning of high-performing societies. They have no individual language and the language used by the managerial elite will be as unintelligible to coal-face managers as Latin was to the laity of fourteenth-century Eisenach before Luther came along. The role of language is fundamental to the process of innovation. If we cannot express a concept or precept, we are unlikely to be able to invent the material object of that idea. Indeed, more fundamentally, if we cannot express our thoughts, the creation of ideas in the first place will be a virtual impossibility.

Language is also fundamental to the basic functionality of a firm. Different groups in a firm will tend to speak very different languages. Marketers will not understand IT people; the finance group will be unintelligible to HR; a board director will speak a foreign language to a shop worker. Each functional discipline has its lingo, its expressive rituals, its syntax. It will reflect not only different training and education, but also a different sense of belonging. Functional silos tend to form societies and members of these societies often have more in common with similar professionals in other firms than with members of different silos within their own firm. The absence of shared identifiers and language is one of the fundamental inefficiencies in firms that reengineering failed to tackle. A company of many languages will not be a society. It will not transfer knowledge efficiently. It will not innovate with fluidity. It will be a Tower of Babel and we all know what happened to that!

Finding the heartland of the firm

The limitations of modern corporate identity are particularly damaging as most firms begin to evolve from being strictly product-based manufacturers and distributors to customer-focused service entities. Most large firms are becoming more like consultants in the way they bundle their product offering with customer services. The communication content has escalated dramatically. This makes language fundamental to the underlying product. If the customer benefit cannot be expressed in a proprietorial and value adding fashion then the product is likely to be effectively worthless.

The firm needs to lessen its obsession with corporate branding which, despite its cost, will not produce sustainable competitive advantage. Instead it should focus its resources on ensuring that it has a language which its employees share in their dealings with each other and with the outside world. The core of language is a common grammar and lexicon. The key words in any language say a lot about what matters to that society – the Eskimo's 48 words for snow are not quite matched by the Englishman's 26 variants of tea! A firm's understanding of what drives value creation should condition the lexicon of that firm. A McKinsey or BCG, whose product is utterly intellectual, have highly evolved languages for describing their value creation process. Of course, the adoption of a means of expression cannot simply be mandated. It presupposes a cohesive educational process, something we shall talk about at length in the next chapter.

An embedded language will condition behaviour because it influences interaction. Identity is a fundamentally social concept. It is about facilitating relationships. Language is a medium to reinforce the moral tenets of the firm. It also promotes innovation as ideas can be universally articulated and understood. Language is a profound source of differentiation because it is intensely competitively defensible. A proprietorial language is hard to copy whereas logos will all tend to gravitate to sameness. Language is a fundamental underpinning of the moral framework any society is built upon and a strong moral framework is harder to assail than Krak des Chevaliers.

10

The origin of species: the history of history

We all have a profound psychological need to feel we have an origin which endorses our present. We all like to think well of our antecedents. It is part of a healthy self-image. Having secure origins gives us the confidence to innovate, to push the envelope. They also give us something to fight to preserve for the future. In an important way, our history gives us a purpose. Intelligent people who do not have family escutcheons and country estates to call their own will inevitably look to identify with a community that supplies a past they can have a legitimate claim upon. Being part of such a past is an essential part of feeling good about our present and passionate about our future. If we lack a secure sense of belonging through our family – which today is so often the case – we look to another group to provide that identification.

This is a need societies have only learnt to harness more recently. The Nation State did not consciously invent the history process until the early nineteenth century and the ascendancy of the great collectors of post-industrial Britain. Thereafter it became central to the identity of nationhood, from Washington to Paris. A self-conscious sense of history is fundamental to modern identity. Nationalism arose as a conscious co-opting of this sentiment. The study of history has emerged as one of the fundamental underpinnings of the modern educational system. It was one of the first subjects that appeared on the national curriculum to supplement the thousand-year infatuation amongst pedagogues with Latin and Greek.

Achieving civilisation means something more than energy, will and creative power. It requires the formation of history. The creation of great societies requires a degree of continuity. The early Norsemen are a glaring example of the cost of disregarding history. Within a hundred years around AD 500 they had subdued much of western Europe, armed with frail, low-sided boats and axes. They even got as far as Persia and inscribed their runic graffiti on the lions at Delos. But these invaders were also in a continual state of flux. They didn't feel the need to look forward beyond the next march or voyage. For this reason it did not occur to them to build stone houses or write books. They made no history. Their permanent mark on modern society is minimal. All that immense energy and will-power is virtually forgotten. That compares emphatically to the birth of law under Edward the Confessor. The moral and legal standards of Anglo-Saxon countries are based on precedent, not absolute statute. We judge ourselves through an accumulation of experience.

History is an organic lesson in self-conduct. Studying our history is an act of perpetual self-confirmation. It binds us to our past and guides us into the future.

As in so many respects, the great religions were way ahead of national society even by the time William put an arrow into Harold's eye. All the great religions are founded on a keen sense of tradition. They are built on the well-trodden stones of what has gone before. Perhaps the most revering of history is Judaism. Judaism is not founded on an idea but an event. It takes the view that the historical context in which life is lived affects one's existence in every way, delineating its problems and its opportunities. All the historical religions – Christianity, Judaism, Islam – which are founded on a concrete event, not a principle, share this same viewpoint. A sense of origin is vital. It provides the centre. Confucianism is similarly steeped in respect for tradition. Confucius asserted the importance of heritage as a counter-thrust to the corrosive loss of social order in the China of his day.

The company is a very different beast. Corporations rarely have a collective memory that goes back more than five years. The advent of each new CEO is the reinvention of the present, usually with an explicit rejection of the past. Analysts barely track a trend beyond two years. Few firms encourage an understanding of their past in order to shape their future. They have no foundation for learning the lessons that the firm has learnt from its past and that no consultant can possibly understand.

There is, on the face of it, a good reason for this. In the corporate context, the sense of pastness has been associated with obsolescence. Most firms that have developed a corporate history have used it as a wall to hide behind. More firms than we can possibly list, from British Leyland in the UK to PanAm in the US, have had venerable histories and all got slammed by markets evolving faster than them. But this is not the full story. The distinction to be drawn is a simple one – it divides between static heritage, 'we did this and therefore . . .' and living heritage, 'we did it once, we know we can do it again and we must do it again . . .'. In its positive manifestations heritage is not a list of values scribed on ageing, mottled parchment; it is not a museum of prototypes; it is not the dusty tomes of ancient board minutes; it is not enshrined in the cigar-stained oak boardroom; it is not scrupulously preserved logotype or escutcheons. These are the trappings of a dead culture; a firm clinging to the past. Living heritage is literally a continual learning process based on precedent.

The grey hair factor

History is based on accumulated knowledge. Knowledge has to come from somewhere. It cannot simply be bought on CD-ROMs or invented by consultants. A firm's history in fact often resides in generations that are no longer core to the day-to-day activity of the business. The older generations of managers have witnessed past successes and failures. They also understand how the business has evolved and how its identity has shifted. This is called long-term benchmarking and it is critical to any society. Any structure which is dominantly social in nature seems intuitively to place a value on life wisdom. Old age has classically been revered by the national character. Confucianism has its Western counterparts.

But the modern firm has on the whole trounced that wisdom. With the effective retirement age in many firms now down to 55, the longest collective experience can be little more than twenty years. 'Retirement' in most firms has become utterly bound up with cost cutting. It is usually a painful severance in which the employee plots to maximise benefits and the firm to minimise liability. It becomes a negotiation in which any real relationship is destroyed. What does it matter after all? That person will no longer be a contributor. Their feelings are largely irrelevant.

On reflection, this cavalier attitude towards the older members of the community is quite extraordinary. It is reminiscent of a society at its most primitive phases of evolution – one where only the fit survive and the old die off. As society has grown more sophisticated it has generally learnt that older members of the community have lessons to teach and that learning such lessons is the only real form of collective advancement. Otherwise each new generation is condemned to start at the beginning again in a Sisyphean repetition. That is why the reverence attached to old age is self-interested, and not just soft-hearted sentimentalism. Firms have not yet learnt to tap this aspect of their resource base. Instead they burn a lot of cash trying to dispense with it. The one set of exceptions is probably the professions – medicine and the barrister trade. No-one messes with a horse-haired judge!

The history lesson

So much of the latent value we have identified in this book is bound up with education. Corporate education presents a problem for most firms. The expense hits the P&L immediately and the benefit only percolates through later in an intangible fashion. Hence, firms only spend half of 1 per cent of their income investing in their human assets – an extraordinary fact if you think about it that way. Capex, by contrast, usually averages between 3 and 5 per cent of revenues. The result has been that executive education has effectively been out-sourced to the MBA schools – a non-proprietorial source of know-how that often creates little tornados that churn through jobs like they were going out of fashion. But what alternative do firms have? The answer to the problem lies within.

The best teachers are often the older generation. Teaching can be done by otherwise retiring members of the firm's community, incurring only minor expense and probably reducing severance payments. Such a strategy also provides a much more fulfilling culmination to a career. The natural career evolution moves from doer to teacher, from knowledge worker to knowledge conveyor. Teachers are perhaps amongst the few people we actually remember during the entire course of our lives. Much like great books, they stay with us because they form part of our personal fabric. Experienced teachers have the luxury of distance and they have the opportunity to prepare based on experience.

Precisely the same is true of course of that other vast, neglected talent pool – recent mothers. The churn of female employees in their mid-thirties is structurally high. It repre-sents a huge drain of talent but it also hits the P&L in the form of statutory maternity leave costs. Most firms are acutely aware of the cost of maternity. A majority of mothers either do not return to their former employer or change their career entirely to accommodate the new demands on their time. This is a fantastic resource lost to the company. As with retirees, the opportunity to harness it on a more flexible basis for teaching is entirely ignored. The potential of maternity leavers as teachers is also interesting in terms of the femi-nine skills such a process will inevitably disseminate. So many of the heartland characteristics of the company are feminine. These feminine facets are way under-represented in most firms, which remain dominated by masculine management style and a paucity of communication skills.

So, if a firm has a ready pool of educators, what should be the nature of the curriculum? History can be stale and desiccated. But it can also be made to live. Living history is populated by heroes – formative events embodied in individual endeavours that have meaning. The historical hero is a moral role model, from Washington to Winston Churchill. In a broader sense, living history is closely bound up with story-telling. Stories bring the past alive, they provide the opportunity to recraft it in a way that makes it relevant to the present. They also engage and humour. People are not motivated by doctrine or abstract ideas of right and wrong. They are motivated by tales of lives to which they can aspire, with which they empathise or which inspire feeling. The process of enactment is a surrogate for living out someone else's life as our own. What at heart matters are not ideas but people, or at least ideas dressed up as people.

Business education is one area where the use of empathy and identification is almost entirely ignored. In virtually every other aspect of education we have learnt to personalise. Business strategy remains adamantly a pseudo-science of boxes, flow charts and numbers. As business is all about relationships and feelings, this clearly is inadequate. The core of any corporate curriculum has to be the delicate art of managing relationships and communications with other people. All else follows.

Finding the heartland of the firm

The modern Nation State has evolved a foundation of history for a reason. Without history we have no cultural root to bind us together as a community. Lack of history robs us of a social framework. The absence of tradition in the US, the lack of a historical example and the paucity of cultural root-edness amongst certain deracinated groups, has undoubtedly contributed to its high level of social turbulence. It has been forced to counter the resulting dysfunctionality with force – a strong CIA, tough cops, crowded jails and the rule of the hand gun enshrined by the NRA. Without history, society breaks into ethnic groups, all the way down to whatever denominator can provide a meaningful sense of heritage.

Of course, the concept of tradition is a difficult one in the Internet age where everything is being invented and revo-lutionised at such a pace, where there appear to be no precedents for what is going to happen next. The term 'tradi-tion' is unfortunately associated with conservatism, defence of the status quo, institutionalisation. Tradition in its true sense denotes a stable platform, guaranteeing enough conti-nuity to allow healthy risk taking and individual endeavour. A level of security and confidence has shown itself to be a necessary precursor to all successful innovation and risk taking.

To provide such a platform of healthy continuity the firm has to develop a curriculum of teaching to embed a sense of the firm's heritage. The best people it has to deliver such a process cost-effectively are often retirees and women on extended maternity leave. The latter, in particular, are ideally suited to disseminating the soft aspects of manage-ment that are so critical to a coherent society. Life is the best teacher.

11

The restless spirit:
the perpetual interrogative

Societies are no different from all working mechanisms – from human beings to car engines. If they are left idle, they decline. The process of asking the difficult questions, of questioning the status quo, is what produces forward movement. Momentum is not the result of a clinical, tightly managed process. It is more usually the output of a somewhat traumatic and heated set of exchanges with ourselves and others. Life's progress is very much akin to a Shakespearean plot – the disruption of one order is a chaotic precursor of another, wiser order. We are all King Lears.

We know that entire civilisations can become petrified and that in order to be regenerated they first have to be destroyed. For 4000 years from 1766 BC to AD 1895 China was ruled by 16 dynasties. A new dynasty began with the rulers carrying out reforms and extending boundaries of Chinese administration. This was followed by a golden age of stability, prosperity and cultural achievement. Then, as routine set in, so would decay. The usual hallmark of incip-ient decay was anxiety on the part of a vested elite to hold on to their existing social order. The dynasty would fall because of internal rebellion, only for the cycle to repeat itself once more.

The great merit of European civilisation is that it has never ceased to develop and change. It has not been based on a perfected form but is the product of competing ideas and inspiration. When Vasari, the Renaissance art historian, asked himself why it was in Florence and not elsewhere that men became cognoscenti in the arts, he gave as his answer, 'The spirit of criticism; the air of Florence making minds naturally free and not content in their mediocrity.' The same DNA has, of course, been sown in American soil and burst into an even more vibrant form of society over the past two hundred years. The intensity of competing ideas is palpable. It is the act of asking questions that produces forward motion in all societies. It is the stifling of questions that ultimately produces rot. The dictators have not learnt the lesson. They by definition never do!

The interrogative flame we so take for granted was nurtured in an improbable place. Nowadays we typically think of religion as reactionary and conformist. In fact, from the Middle Ages the Church was a seedbed of exploration. The main structure, the Christian faith, was unshakable. But round it arose a play of minds, an intellectual feat of acro-batics, that has hardly been equalled since. As Abelard, the great intellectual prize-fighter of Paris, put it, 'I must under-stand in order that I may believe. By doubting we come to questioning and by questioning we perceive the truth.' The fact that, despite his apparent iconoclasm, he survived to die of old age at Cluny in 1142 says something of the tolerance of the institution of the Church at the time.

In an important way, religions are there to encourage such questions to be asked and to act as a methodology through which answers can at least partially be worked towards. Religion is the most serious attempt made by humanity to infer from the mess in which we find ourselves the great pattern that threads through it all. It recognises that the worthwhile aspects of reality – its values, meaning and purpose – evade the crisp solutions proposed by science in the same way that rainbows always elude the hiker. Instead we must settle for fewer easy answers; more grey; tougher demands on our intellect, on our faith. The way to find a path is to ask questions, to face our doubts, to dismiss our prejudices. Inquiry is part of the solution. It opens our minds to new opportunities. Buddhism, perhaps most notably, propounds the positivism of enquiry; enquiry is growth. We are freed from the pain of clutching for permanence if we accept the continual process of change, if we ask the tough questions without fear of being unsettled by the lack of clear answers.

This heritage of self-questioning gave rise to the European rivalries that have fuelled scientific inventiveness ever since. It was only when the Nation State learned to harness the interrogative that it achieved maturity in the form that is so familiar to us today. Debate is, of course, at the heart of the political process. It is the foundation of democracy – that government is answerable to its citizens, that the process of government is founded on a system of checks and balances preserved through political debate. The uncomfortable process of debate has been fought by nascent oligarchs but resistance never endures. Once the hare of questioning is loosed it cannot be recaptured.

Intolerant order

Most firms are intensely nervous about open debate. There is a low tolerance for ambiguity. Rather than asking, they are more comfortable answering. Order is a profound psychological need for most managers, as it is in any environment where the presiding mindset is one of control and measurement. Even though more enlightened management teams have recognised that a healthy, somewhat chaotic internal dialogue is essential to innovation, intuitively control has somehow always been too tempting to resist. That is after all what management is all about, surely?

Innovation is treated by most firms as a discrete process to be managed through a separate protocol. The concept of the R&D department, of the innovation group locked in a facility some way from the main area of production, is symptomatic of the desire on the part of senior management to ring-fence the anarchy of the innovation process, to stop it from infecting the stable work flows of the core business. Curiously enough, the same is true even of the creative departments of most advertising agencies. This paradigm, that preserves the stable core and removes any source of self-questioning, is replicated in the departmental structure of most organisations. Keeping all the marketers together and separate from the production and IT groups ensures that each focuses narrowly on the task at hand and the machine remains in balance.

Tolerating debate is not an easy thing for a firm to do. Most firms recognise that those closest to the coal-face or in improbable parts of the organisation have great ideas. But the natural corollary of fostering debate is accountability. That is when the pill really gets bitter. Empowering employees with the right to make fundamental judgements about aspects of the firm's performance is anathema to most management teams. All CEOs are answerable to shareholders who in one form or another are represented on the board. What they are not used to is answerability to their own staff and managers. The boards of most firms are more like ivory towers than Oxford ever was!

Of course, giving employees the right to question also gives them ownership. Accountability of the firm to staff and managers means they become de facto guardians of company interests. Give them ownership and they tend to care. It is one of the fundamental rules of property. As soon as people care more about each other and the society they live in then great things usually happen.

Ownership in this sense is not something the average firm has embraced outside the professional partnership. The most the average firm does to poll opinion is the annual temperature check through an employee satisfaction survey. These are invariably little more than placebos. The same is true of the infamous focus group which usually amounts to little more than an intensely artificial and embarrassed shuffle between people who are neurotically guarded. There is no accountability. The only real tool the firm is left with is the stock option which again assumes that the only real motivation is cash – the shareholder motive.

Interestingly enough, despite all the talk of shareholder activism, the same insecurity is reflected in the external communications processes of most firms. All public firms have annual general meetings that are meant to be public forums. But on the whole they are more form than substance. Typically, few shareholders actually attend – just a few eccentrics who ask bizarre questions. The real inquiry happens with key institutional shareholders behind closed doors. Interestingly, there is no internal equivalent of the AGM, probably

out of fear that it would deteriorate into a bun-fight. But institutionalising debate and accountability can only be done in
open forum. The firm is just like the human. Insecurity breeds
failure to attack problems openly. Insecurity is the fundamental source of terminal social rot.

Quieting the disquieting
inner voice

Rather than institutionalising debate, the onus has been
thrust upon the individual to solve their own problems. Part
of the individualisation of society is attributable to the rise
of the doctrine of self-accountability. Ever since the popu-
larisation of Freud, there has been an increasing shift towards
self-questioning as a route to self-understanding. Modern
psychology has exchanged the cathartic impulse to confess,
that is at the heart of religious experience, with the excruciating introspection of self-analysis. Self-analysis, even if
administered by a shrink, is ostensibly a solitary activity. It
is premised on self-betterment through personal confrontation. The religious urge to confess is a fundamentally social
one. It does not focus on the personal cure. It focuses on
sharing and openness – on the social balm. Modern thought
has herded us down the solitary path.

Debate is a fundamentally different form of questioning.
It is intensely social in nature. It focuses on communal not
personalised issues. It therefore tends to produce change
which is relevant to a society rather than just one individual.
Contemporary values of competitiveness and benchmarking
encourage self-inquiry which, of course, readily prompts self-
doubt. As Andy Grove of Intel articulated the sentiment,
'only the neurotic survive'. At the centre of most managers'

interrogatives is therefore, not surprisingly, 'what's in it for me', not 'how can we together improve the way we do things'. Firms focus their efforts on rewarding individual effort. The result is questioning that is not necessarily constructive to the society of the firm, although it may advance individual careers. The failure to find social solutions can also mean that the neurotic impulse becomes corrosive to the collective energy of the firm.

Let the knowledge flow

Constructive debate, of course, presupposes knowledge – one of our Socratic moral imperatives. Most firms are intensely guarded about their information. They starve people of critical data. One of the hottest-selling intranet applications is the firewall. This data control mindset is antediluvian. In the Web age information leaks everywhere. If you want to find something out with enough determination, you usually can.

Firms also tend to overemphasise the importance of data. Their neurosis about guarding it like the jewels in the Tower is misplaced. Formalised information is not what really matters in the first place. The value of data on servers is often a fallacy propagated by IT firms selling their databases. Information means nothing unless it is converted into knowledge. Knowledge only exists in the minds of people, not computer hard drives. The real risk for firms lies in losing knowledgeable people who have synthesised data over long periods of time, not in losing the data itself.

This turns the equation on its head. If knowledge is people-dependent, rather than guarding and policing it internally firms should be anxious that it be disseminated as widely as possible and, more importantly, assimilated by as many people as possible within the firm. The risk of leakage to the external community is far outweighed by the risk of key people walking out without having shared what they know with others beforehand. Dissemination ironically enough is the surest line of defence. A culture of dissemination means a culture of debate and debate based on information. Informed debate is what produces great innovation. The fact that aggregate spend on internal communications by corporate America is less than 1 per cent of the spend on external communications suggests that this has not yet been taken seriously!

The Worker Wide Web

Of course, formalised internal communications, controlled, edited and packaged, are not the way to foster positive idea exchange. All firms have networks – indeed they have many different networks. Some of these will be formalised, for example a specific collaborative mechanism to link the marketing and R&D group, enshrined in monthly meetings or team briefings. Other networks will be informal, cutting across departments and even running between the firm itself and its external partners. These informal networks will almost certainly be much more powerful than any formal communications process the firm may have instituted. They will be the source of most people's information about what is really happening in the firm. They will probably carry much more credence than formal communication channels pumping out the party line.

The growth of IT networks has heralded probably the single biggest change to corporations in the past twenty years. Not only has it influenced the nature of a firm's relationships with its external audiences, it has fundamentally altered the power of internal networks. There has been an explosion in the penetration of intranets, originally using proprietary software such as Lotus Notes and, more recently, Web-based technologies. This has ushered in a complete revolution in the way employees communicate with each other across both departments and geographies. In essence, it has acted to reinforce and amplify the informal networks that already existed. The ability of senior management to control the flow of information between employees is now absolutely non-existent. Such networks cannot be policed.

By far the most common on-line application is e-mail, not database access or use of the complex, engineered content that populates most corporate websites. The interesting thing about e-mail-based communication is that it tends to cross departmental and hierarchical boundaries better than any other medium, principally because it is personal rather than formal. The PC is a highly intimate item for most executives, housing personal files and addresses. The great thing about an e-mail message is that it downloads directly on to this personal medium. Whilst a secretary might check it on behalf of their boss, their willingness to review it as a gatekeeper will be lower. Nor is it subject to editing like normal formal content.

Given that it is an irresistible force, companies are making a big mistake in resisting rather than harnessing the informal flow of information. Knowledge is created by intelligent people in a company engaging in debate. It is no longer live knowledge when stored on a server. At that point it is dead and fixed, like a butterfly collection. Debate is positive. It is at its most positive if informed and if it occurs within a framework that makes emerging ideas actionable.

Pay-day

This all of course has a profound implication for incentives – that underpinning of the modern corporation. Virtually all contemporary incentive schemes are based on individual performance. On the whole, amongst more mature members of the corporate community, incentive schemes inspire caution and reservedness – do not express your doubts, do not rock the boat, do not take excessive risks. When one is measured alone, then risks are tough to take. Most of us are not natural gamblers when mortgages and school fees are at stake. It is only when efforts are collective that risks are more readily undertaken. The great social advances are made through cooperative action not solitary effort. The reverse is perhaps true of purely intellectual advancements. But social events are almost always necessary to bring great ideas to life.

The compensation process is a thorny, opaque mystery in most firms. Again, it principally acts to compound the individualisation of motives. It strangles the exchange of information. Why share when all that matters is personal performance? The underlying neurosis is that others might gain competitive advantage by access to one's own details. There has been some movement forward in terms of measurement. The 360° assessment methodology and the Balanced Scorecard both introduce the critical element of peer review and dilute the subjective flaw inherent in top-down assessment. The advent of the option as an element of the pay packages of more senior people also blends motives. But most compensation schemes remain profoundly divisive. At heart, for a firm to be innovative it has to positively reward dissemination of ideas. The most competitive organisation is likely to be one of nascent writers neurotic to gain acceptance of their inventions!

Finding the heartland of the firm

Most firms base their product or service advantage on a static view of innovation. A breakthrough is made, commercialised and it is on this that the firm survives for potentially decades. Such a system favours a functional view of innovation – the classic R&D group, the creative department. It was conceived from the Adamsian functional vision of specialisation. The role of management is to impose a formal process on the disturbingly anarchic minds of the boffins.

A much surer route to innovation is not to do away with the greenhouses or the labs but to take down their walls and allow the debate to extend through the entire organisation. Innovation is a characteristic of an inquisitive, intellectually restless society, not a tightly controlled one.

The real barriers to debate in most firms are the old dams of departmental competence. Most firms are still divided into specialisms, from finance through to marketing. Professionals buried in the nomenclature of their specialisation often miss the big picture which to the outsider is so glaringly obvious. Collapsing these into teams was one of the tenets of the reengineering movement. It didn't work. Specialism is necessary, given the complexity of modern business needs, and like-minded people need to be together to create sparks. But equally, groups cannot be isolated from one another. They need to share information and ideas. We have already explored the issue of shared language. Firms also need to remove barriers to information flow. Part of that process is instituting lateral accountability. Lateral accountability means one group ensuring they deliver what another needs and, if not, taking the rap for the failure.

This also means a fundamental change to the concept of what constitutes management. Senior managers will have to move away from their comfortable roles as chess players to roles as facilitators. They will also have to move away from the endemic use of spies – alias old-style management consultants – to enforce their notions of structure and help plan their moves of the chess pieces. The role of governance becomes one of managing debate and consensus.

So our reconfigured board has another set of challenges. It has to foster debate, it has to free the flow of information and hence it must move from a position of control to one of facilitation. Communication with the organisation is based on informal networks not excruciating formal protocols. The process is not owned by a department, it is common property. There are no thought police. Ideas belong to no man.

12

Positive thinking: things can only get better

The birth of any civilisation requires a modicum of prosperity and stability – enough to provide a little leisure. But far more fundamentally it requires confidence – confidence amongst citizens in the society in which they live, belief in its philosophy, credence in its laws and collective confidence in one's own mental powers. The advents of such moments of collective confidence are epiphanies in the history of humanity. They are not the norm. History has been scattered with such epiphanies when society appears to have gained the strength to cohere. One such time was around 3000 BC when civilisation suddenly emerged simultaneously in Egypt, Mesopotamia and the Indus Valley. Another was around the year AD 1100 with the birth of the great Gothic movements in places like Chartres and Durham. And perhaps most spectacular of them all, in 1400 the Renaissance burst into flower. The dazzling summit of human achievement represented by Michelangelo, Raphael and Leonardo da Vinci lasted for less than twenty years. Great civilisations, just like great companies, appear to carry the seeds of their own destruction!

If one asks why Greece, Rome or Florence collapsed, the real answer is that after an explosion of cooperative energy they were left exhausted. Even the first invaders of the Roman Empire in turn became exhausted and succumbed to the same weakness as the people they conquered. They lost forward momentum. The same is true of all societies, including the corporation. A period of explosive energy over perhaps two decades, born of collective enthusiasm, becomes mired in organisational complexity as the emphasis shifts from creating to managing. The shift to management inevitably leads to the path of preservation of vested interests, to secure what has already been created.

The beginning of the end is usually signalled by continual efforts to rekindle the flame by switching senior management teams. But any amelioration is usually temporary if the organisation itself is sclerotic. The challenge is how to keep the creative positivism systematically embedded. Before 1850 it is hard to find any evidence of a successful formula. The modern democracy is only a hundred and fifty years old, so is not necessarily the ultimate test case. Other than religion, however, it is the best role model of a self-revitalising social structure that we have.

The only more enduring source of organised positivism is religion. All the great religions assure us that if we could see the full picture we would find it more integrated, more wonderful than we suppose. This vision of a beatific order, slightly beyond the grasp of our comprehension, inspired the

Elysian landscapes of Giotto, the aerial frescos of Michelangelo. It has made people over the centuries stretch their
intellects to reach new heights. If things are pervaded by a
grand design, they are not only more integrated, they are also
better than they seem. There lies in this assurance the hope
of a better personal state worth fighting for – a redemption.
Redemption is the principal goal of all the great religions;
the movement towards a better, a happier state of being.
Perhaps the most forward-thrusting religion of them all is
Judaism. Judaism tends to assume that the fault originated
from ourselves and not from the stars. Hence it demands a
creative response. That notion of self-determinism is at the
heart of positivism. Fatalism assumes predestiny.

The power of simplicity

Social positivism is almost always associated with a clear,
simple goal that is intelligible to everyone. The discovery of
crystallising, simple goals has marked the progress of civilisation. After the fall of Rome, civilisation appeared to have
ended. Humanity might have drifted downwards indefinitely
but for the fact that, in the middle of the seventh century,
there appeared a new force, with a faith and a will to conquer
lesser cultures. The strength of Islam lay in its simplicity. The
early Christian Church had dissipated its strength by
becoming embroiled in theological controversies, carried on
for three centuries with excruciating ingenuity. But Muham-
mad, the Prophet of Islam, preached the simplest doctrine
that has ever gained acceptance. Within fifty years the classical world was overrun. If a vision is clear enough and
compelling enough, bright people have a wonderful habit of
finding the inner resources to fight for it, even if the path is

stony and obstructed. An analogous stripping away was to be achieved by Martin Luther seven centuries on, in the face of a sclerotic, obsessive, ritualised Catholicism that meant little to everyday folk.

Simplification usually means purging. Over time all societies are apt to swaddle themselves in complication, until ultimately all forward motion is strangled. The exorcising of such sclerosis can be bloody. As Thomas Jefferson put it, 'The tree of liberty must be refreshed from time to time with the blood of patriots and tyrants.' Freedom of speech, belief, expression and movement unlock tremendous energy. But such energy can at times be terrifying and even destructive to the existing order. Edmund Burke's 'wild gas of liberty' has explosive potential.

History has taught us that the beginning of each social epiphany is characterised by the emergence of iconoclasts. In the commercial world we call them entrepreneurs! Most firms are bad at tolerating iconoclasts and at recognising epiphanies when they are about to happen. Most firms are also bad at simplification and creating clear, emotive goals. Corporate strategy as a discipline usually imposes a rule book. It is formalistic and mechanistic. It is also typically intensely complicated. That is how the strategy consultants of the world justify their fees! That is not positivism. It is symptomatic of the paranoia we so often mistake for management.

The principle of self-betterment

Positivism is founded on the principle of self-betterment. In social epiphanies people find a voice to improve their lot through collective action. Once that possibility for redemption becomes mired in the anxiety of incumbents to preserve the status quo, the optimism fades and with it the epiphany itself.

The democratic Nation State is unusually endowed with structural positivism. No other institution invests as much energy and resource convincing its population of the possibility for self-improvement. Part of this is pure marketing, the sort of self-publicity that gets a government re-elected. But, more constructively, to justify itself government has to find areas of national activity where it can make a difference. It has to deliver tangible betterment. Every meeting of Parliament or the Senate is about finding a better way.

As we have already discussed, it is a fundamental moral principle that the pursuit of happiness is a legitimate aim for humanity. The Nation State enshrines this principle at its core. By contrast, the average firm is virtually oblivious to the concept. The objective is single-mindedly betterment of shareholders in the immediate term while the factors of production come second. It is the classic cart before the horse. The best surety of performance is that employees have a clear place to get to which will deliver them a better lot in life. At its most abstract, healthy firms, like organisms, need to have an organic objective of growth and propagation. In essence this urge replicates on a collective scale the impulse of more influential members to expand their own horizons and exercise the ambit of their egos. And that is a good thing.

The feel-good factor

It is a well-recognised phenomenon that the better consumers feel the more they will spend. This concept is encapsulated in the 'feel-good factor', an elusive construct tracked doggedly by the forecasters. The same is of course true for employees. The more positively they feel about the future, the more willing they will be to invest energy in an undertaking. How good are the vibes in a company? How positive does its population feel about the future and how actively are its members prepared to invest in that future? These are questions the analysts rarely, if ever, ask. They are something the average mid-level manager asks themselves daily.

Most corporations are 'expectant' – their principal instinct is to drive towards improvement. However, that sentiment is all too often only relevant to the members of the board and a relatively small number of senior managers, all of whom will have the acute incentive of seeing the stock price rise. For this group of people the fruits of positivism are very sweet! By contrast, most normal employees have increasingly focused on what they might lose through change, whether through restructuring or downsizing. Their frame of reference is negative. The status quo is good. Intrapreneurship might sound catchy but it is anathema to most when the dominant frame of mind is 'Oh my God, what the hell do I do if I miss a mortgage payment?'

The optimistic frame of mind is something that typically distinguishes start-up ventures from large corporations. The atmosphere of euphoric expectation in smaller entrepreneurial firms, where everyone shares in the excitement, is partly why they usually experience more impressive growth rates. Most large firms can only look on with a mixture of contempt and envy at the messianic motivation of the up-starts snapping at their heels and wait for them to fall in turn into the corporate strategy trap.

The conventional and ubiquitous definition of progress in terms of metrics such as share price and EPS fundamentally misses the emotional point. To feel good about themselves, most people need to feel that they are contributing to building something admirable. The goal is not abstract. It is connected with gaining admiration and social respect. We are going somewhere and we are getting there together. The motive is fundamentally social in nature. This is why team sports are so compelling. The heroes they produce are the product of group success. It is also why start-ups led by charismatic individuals tend to elicit greater enthusiasm from their employees.

A universal condition of social epiphanies is based on just such a movement from individual to collective ambition. Gratification of mature ambitions is fundamentally social. We wish to be seen to have contributed and excelled at those deeds the community values. This need for endorsement we all share, whether we are a knowledge worker or shop-floor mechanic. Without that context positivism is not possible, unless we are psychopathic misanthropes! Without that context it is also hard for us to take the risks that are a precursor to innovation. Making tough calls alone constitutes risk. Taken together as a group, the same choice becomes exciting. The pure entrepreneur willing to bet the farm is a rare beast. But great firms take great risks with vast amounts of capital at stake. That is one of the benefits of acting as a large social group.

Finding the heartland of the firm

Most firms are gripped by an introverted obsession with strategy, few by an expansionist sense of mission and zeal. The question is how do established, long-standing firms replicate the same energy of their youthful counterparts? Thirty years into a marriage how is the stimulus resparked? The same question dogs every institution in its middle years, through from marriage to corporate management.

In order to persuade employees and managers that the future is worth fighting for, they need a clear understanding that they are heading to a better place, that getting there will be rewarding and that it has meaning for them. It cannot simply be about improving shareholder value, even if that is the requisite by-product. The abstract financial goals of most senior management teams are not relevant and certainly not compelling for the average manager or employee. The goals need to be clearly articulated and to explicitly offer them a means of self-betterment. That self-betterment need not simply be financial. The most motivating path is one of improving skills and capability. We return to education as inevitably as a river runs to the sea! The successful society will have optimism sewn into its character through an endless process of self-improvement. We all long to recreate ourselves, to live out our dreams. Companies should provide that opportunity.

13

Lady Enigma:
the hunger for forbidden
fruit

Mystery is at the heart of all human progress. It conditions our aspirations. Once something is fully understood it is conquered. It is human nature to have a lesser regard for something that has been conquered. It inspires no awe. The fables of salvation, of acts of redemption, the possibility of the miraculous – all have fed a thirst for that possibility. Mystery is also intimately bound up with social inclusion. Societies create mysteries to lend themselves awe and add value to the privilege of membership.

The modern Nation State is founded on cultivated myth. The formation of the US has been one of the most self-conscious acts of myth making. The design of Washington on the grand formal lines laid out by L'Enfant, populated with the vast white monuments to Washington, Lincoln and

Jefferson, and those echoing words of the Declaration of
Independence, 'We hold these truths to be self-evident . . .'
– all created a myth to sanctify the invention of civilisation
in the wilderness. And it worked! For the immigrants from
the Old World the myth of the New World was the magnetic
force that drew them towards it, from Ireland, Sicily and
Poland. The New World had of course learnt its tricks from
the Old. Post-revolutionary France turned the fall of the
Bastille into a heroic event personified by Madame Liberty
manning the ramparts. In fact the Bastille only held half a
dozen old men who didn't even want to be let out. Bare-
breasted Britannia aboard her oceanic chariot was a figment
of the Georgian imagination to fuel maritime conquest with
missionary zeal.

The Nation State was only tapping into a phenomenon
that the Church had been cultivating for over a thousand
years. Religions have always traded in mystery – the mystery
of how Christ could possibly have made water turn to wine
or risen from the dead; who exactly was Lao-tzu; how
Confucius could possibly have unified China in a single
human lifetime. Reality is steeped in ineluctable mystery; that
problem which for the human mind has no solution – like
the astrophysical world where the more we understand its
formulation the stranger the universe becomes. Since it is
not rationally comprehensible, participation calls for belief.
Once people believe, they are already surrendering their individualism to a social force bigger than themselves.

Who's afraid of the unknown?

Most management teams are intensely mistrusting of the
myths they inherit when they assume office. They focus on

exorcising the ghosts. In the wake of the core competency movement, there has been an obsession with increasing transparency – so that value can be understood clearly by analysts. The concomitant by-product is an obsession with measurement – from financial indices to surveys of employee satisfaction. Measurement-based systems all inevitably gravitate to a norm. After all, without norms measurement means nothing.

As a result the individual quirkiness of companies has been eclipsed by increasing homogeneity. Most significant firms in a given sector have similar products, similar strategies, comparable management philosophies and even shared clients. With the surge in consolidation activity there is also increasing homogeneity of size. At one end of the scale there is a small cadre of global consolidators and at the other the huddle of local market niche players, with increasingly little in-between. The result is chronic difficulty in achieving differentiation and an intense and unrelenting squeeze on margins, which in turn compel them to grow endlessly through acquisition to sustain earnings growth. There is an inexorable gravitation towards a grey corporate mean.

A key risk of such homogeneity is what it means for individual employees. Successful societies are those that people want to join. They also tend to be those that are tough to join – back to the old Groucho Marx chestnut, 'I wouldn't join a club that would take me as a member.' The circle of exclusivity is self-reinforcing. The social strategy of exclusivity is akin to the market strategy of differentiation. You attract customers and induce them to pay a premium because they believe that they are partaking of something exclusive that reinforces their sense of self-worth and social standing. Inducing talented employees to undertake commitment to a firm is no different. There is a reason that the majority of graduates from places like Harvard and Insead compete to gain access to McKinsey and BCG, and continued to do so even at the height of the Dotcom frenzy. Such societies are opaque, their private networks are legendary, their culture is exclusive. For public companies to achieve that status is, of course, far more challenging. But it is possible.

The aura of value creates value. It also seeps through inexorably into the investment community. If an institutional shareholder believes the firm is capable of extraordinary things he cannot yet apprehend, he will typically take a longer view of the stock. This alleviates an enormous pressure created by quarterly trading churn. The ten-month infatuation with Web stocks during 1999 and early 2000, where even the most basic questions were disregarded in the love affair with infinite growth, is one extreme example of suspension of critical faculties in the name of pure faith. The long run of investment into Long Term Capital Management illustrates the point even more starkly. Supposedly sophisticated investors were literally twisting arms to put cash into a fund that was doing nothing more than taking unhedged bets on currency movements. More positively, Berkshire Hathaway has sustained its mystique for almost thirty years and has had one of the most stable investor bases in corporate America. Myth moves mountains, including mountains of cash.

The stronger the sense of mystique surrounding a firm, the more membership of it confers status, imbues a sense of belonging, and the more possibilities it holds for those lucky enough to participate. The more mystique surrounds it, the more value is likely to be attributed to it. It might just do something amazing. The corporate equivalent of mystery is 'goodwill' – the packet of value that comes from no clear source and which is intangible. The greater the goodwill of the corporation, the less easily it will be understood, the more brain power, mystery and magic must be attributable to it. Up to 80 per cent of the value of modern firms such as Microsoft, Dell, Omnicom or WPP is in goodwill. It is something even the accountants are getting more comfortable with. The rise of goodwill has occurred almost exactly in tandem with the shift of value added from capital to talent. The greater the percentage of goodwill the more 'with it' the firm is likely to be.

Finding the heartland of the firm

Inspiring awe is largely a communication process. The world needs to see enough to gauge that what they can't see must be pretty impressive. McKinsey produces its quarterly business review of innovative thinking but it charges a million a shot for full frontal access. The mistake many firms make is thinking that mailshots and PR will cut the mustard. Myth evolves through informal networks, not through advertising. It is built up through its membership. McKinsey's *Quarterly* is geared primarily to its membership.

The organic, non-formalistic nature of this process also implies a very different management style. To inspire awe, managers in general have to acquire a tolerance for ambiguity. There has to be a movement away from detailed strategies. There also has to be a focus on people. Clubs are only as good as their membership. Their power is not measured by the age of their building or the size of the billiard room!

In our discussion of language we talked about the development of grammar and key terms. In our discussion of the historical perspective of the company we talked about the celebration of seminal events in the company's history. All institutions imbued with mystique need such seminal material to bind them together. They form the motif that runs through everything that touches the society of the firm. The axis point of myth is often some seminal event in that creation of the society – winning back from the brink. Britain was rescued from oblivion at Dunkirk by a flotilla of small craft. The nascent America was reprieved from annihilation at the hands of superior forces by Washington's last-ditch crossing at Valley Forge. Such events give birth to myth. Few firms have anything as potent. Few firms have a motif of formative events around which people can cluster. Few firms cultivate their human networks. Few firms understand the role of myth. That is one reason why most firms find differentiation so hard.

14

Differentiation or death: fortifying the heartland of the firm

Most larger firms are being slowly strangled by declining margins in their core businesses. The product of convergence towards sameness has been commoditisation, and it has affected every sector, from PCs through to legal services. The biggest challenge firms face is how to differentiate and therefore raise profitability. A vast army of consultants has focused on benchmarking performance and that has ironically been a contributor to the disease of homogeneity. What is clear going forward is that differentiation is dependent on intangibles – customer service, marketing, creativity, etc. – which means it is dependent on people. Roughly 80 per cent of manufacturing value added is in the product's name, merchandising and R&D. People of course present a whole new challenge – grouped together they present a social

Figure 14.1   Universal attributes of a competitive society

challenge. That means new benchmarking is called for –
social benchmarking.

The two most pervasive and enduring models of social
organisation are the organised religions and the Nation State.
We explored the former in *Reinspiring the Corporation*. In
exposing the fundamental underpinning of the Nation State,
we have found that the core social characteristics are similar.
This would suggest there is a fairly universal set of attributes
that make any society competitive, namely:

- An evolving and powerful framework of moral authority.
- A mutually supportive context focused on collective outcomes.
- A highly developed common language, idiom and identity.
- A clear and powerful sense of heritage and purpose.
- A continual flow of self-questioning.
- A positive, even aggressive, view of the future.
- An enduring mystique.

The way to secure a powerful community appears to be to establish a strong moral framework, where individual priorities are satisfied through group objectives, where there is a unifying and unique shared language, where a process of education keeps the flame of heritage alive, where exchange of ideas and dialogue is intense (even to the point of self-questioning), although always within a context of positive ambition for self-betterment, and where membership of the club confers a status no-one would willingly or rationally forgo.

Achieving this balance poses a real challenge for the average company. Despite the rise of goodwill as the principal source of accrual-based value, firms are still largely entrenched in a capital intensive mindset. Corporate strategy still lays down rigid rules. The strategic impetus of most firms has been to simplification and narrowing of focus. The main application of IT investment has been for enhanced financial control. At heart the machine is geared to respond to quarterly inspection. The dream of greatness is deflated in favour of quarterly reliability. Most firms are beginning to bang up against the limitations of this strait-jacket. The imperative is for growth and margin enhancement, both of which can only be achieved through differentiation. That fact is becoming well recognised but few firms have gone the next step towards grasping that competitive advantage therefore lies in their ability to manage themselves as societies – that social functionality is the ultimate source of differentiation.

Rather than learning from the national model, the average firm is simply subject to it. The firm is still fundamentally tied to the Nation State. In order to develop, firms have to achieve an identity separate from their home state. The question-mark hanging over the relevance of the nation should make it easier for firms to form their own societies – to sever the umbilical cord. If corporations are having a tough time differentiating themselves, the average Nation State has just as daunting a task in competing to attract FDI. The world is full of a cluttered miscellany of nations which are very hard to distinguish between. Who after all can tell apart Tajikstan, Kyrgyzstan, Turkmenistan, Kazakhstan and Uzbekistan?

The key tools available to countries to attract FDI – tax incentives, regulatory relief and preferred land arrangements – are available to all governments. They are not a source of differentiation. At the same time the bipolar world of Europe and the US is increasingly less relevant in global consumption terms. In 1990 the US, Europe and ex-USSR accounted for 30 per cent of the world population. By 1990 this was 20 per cent and by 2050 it will be 10 per cent. Of course, this will at least for the foreseeable future be offset by relative spending power. In 1995 per capita income in the hundred or so mid-income countries was just over $1000 whereas that of the 25 rich countries was nearly $25 000. But the international balance will be a more insecure and shifting one.

This new order may in fact pose real challenges for world stability. George Soros has already pronounced his eulogy for the Western market system: 'I can already discern the makings of the final crisis. It will be political in character. Indigenous political movements are likely to arise that will seek to expropriate the multinational corporations and recapture the national wealth.'[4] Whilst this may be a little melodramatic, it is likely that the level of local instability will increase. As Lenin envisioned presciently in 1917:

> Half a century ago Germany was a miserable, insignificant country, as far as its capitalist strength was concerned, compared with the strength of England at the time. Japan was similarly insignificant compared to Russia. Is it conceivable that in twenty years time the relative strength of the great powers will remain unchanged? Absolutely inconceivable.

There will remain the tension between the nation's existence in an aggressive military political world and its existence in a laissez-faire economic world, a tension between its search for military security and economic security. As MacKinder has warned us, 'The great wars of history are the outcome, indirect or direct, of the unequal growth of nations.'

Amid this imbroglio the social role of corporate society is potentially a moderating one. In 1938, after all, it was the capitalist states that were the most anxious to avoid war, and capitalists were the class most opposed to conflict, including in Germany. Corporations certainly have the advantage that they are more efficient at forming global alliances and acquiring international capability than countries. The rate of economic integration amongst the top five hundred global corporates far outstrips the political integration of Nation States. In twenty years or so the world population will number eight to nine billion, multiplying the intensity of

---

[4] See Soros, George. *The Crisis of Global Capitalism. Open Society Endangered.* Little, Brown, 1998.

global interaction by a factor of six relative to what it was in 1900. The global firm is probably the only institution with the nimbleness to harness that variety. The fumblings of the EC have amply demonstrated that countries are not up to the task. But to play such a role, and to possess the power to do so, the firm will have to strengthen its functionality as a social unit. Unless it is strong socially, it will remain a short-lived investor 'play' only.

The growth in retail investor sophistication, of IPOs and buy-outs, has fostered a view of companies as tradable assets. The American dream is to raise private equity to fuel a start-up, achieve an IPO and then a personal exit before moving on to the next one. This poses the inevitable question, what is a corporation? What is there to balance the prevailing bias of viewing the firm as nothing more than a punt? Morality is based on a sense of belonging to a community, be it family, friends, tribe, nation or humanity. A market economy does not constitute a community. Nor does a private equity play.

But we cannot afford to be idealistic or liberal-minded. Social scientists often point to the paternalistic corporations of the world as the role models of the future. Tata, India's largest company, operates in hotels, steel, trucks, electronics and defence. It takes a paternalistic view of its responsibility to the communities it employs. Its steel town at Jamshedpur is a paragon of order and fairness amidst the corruption of the poverty-stricken state of Bihar. A hundred and fifty years ago the Quaker institutions of Cadbury and Lever Brothers were doing the same thing in Victorian Britain. Kellogg's and The Quaker Company were reforming the nature of employ-ment on the eastern seaboard. But times have changed. Competition has changed. Philanthropy cannot viably form the heart of successful business, however nice it would be to propose that it should do so. Social cohesion is not about philanthropy. It is about competitiveness. It is in fact probably the only reliable source of differentiation left to western firms.

We began our exploration of the heartland of the firm with the map-makers. The fundamental limitation of the analogy of map-making is that it is bound by physical space. The society of the Nation State is defined by physical boundaries. The global firm has the chance to dispense with those limitations and create its own maps – maps of its own social network, the shape and spread of which will be unique to each firm. That means each firm can, if it chooses, be a Columbus or a da Gama. There is no need to assume the world has been discovered. Discovery is a social affair and most global societies are yet to be discovered!

Select
bibliography

Arnott, Dave. *Corporate Cults: The Insidious Lure of the All Consuming Corporation*. Amacom, 2000.

Austin, James E. *Managing in Developing Countries: Strategic Analysis and Operating Techniques*. The Free Press, 1990.

Baldock, Robert. *The Last Days of the Giants? A Routemap for Big Business Survival*. John Wiley & Sons, 2000.

Belasco, James, and Jerre Stead. *Soaring with the Phoenix: Renewing the Vision, Reviving the Spirit and Re-creating the Success of Your Company*. Warner Books, 1999.

Bennett, S. Stewart III, and Joel M. Stern. *The Quest for Value: The EVA Management Guide*. Harper Business, 1987.

Bower, Joseph L., and Clayton M. Christensen. 'Disruptive Technologies: Catching the Waves.' *Harvard Business Review*, January/ February 1995.

Camp, Robert C. *Benchmarking: The Search for Industry Best Practices that Lead to Superior Performance*. Quality Press, 1989.

Campbell, Andrew, Michael Goold, and Marcus Alexander. *Corporate Level Strategy: Creating Value in the Multi-Business Company*. John Wiley & Sons, 1994.

Champy, James. *Reengineering Management: The Mandate for New Leadership*. Harper Business, 1995.

Clark, Kenneth. *Civilisation*. Harper and Row, 1969.

Clausewitz, Carl Von. *On War*. Penguin, 1983.

Copeland, Tom, and Tim Koller. *Valuation: Measuring and Managing the Value of Companies*. 2nd edition. John Wiley & Sons, 1994.

Cragg, Kenneth. *The House of Islam*. Wadsworth, 1988.

Danner, Victor. *The Islamic Tradition*. Amity House, 1988.

Darwin, Charles Gatton. *The Next Million Years*. Doubleday, 1953.

Davenport, Thomas H., and Laurence Prusak. *Working Knowledge: How Organisations Manage What They Know*. HBS Press, 1998.

Davidson, Bill, and Stan Davis. *2020 Vision: Transforming Your Business Today To Succeed Tomorrow*. Simon and Schuster, 1991.

Davis, Stan. *Future Perfect*. Addison Wesley, 1987.

De Geus, Arie. *The Living Company: Growth, Learning and Longevity in Business*. Nicholas Brealey Publishing, 1997.

Freemantle, David. *What Customers Like About You: Adding Emotional Value for Service Excellence and Competitive Advantage*. Nicholas Brealey Publishing, 1998.

Friedheim, Cyrus. *The Trillion Dollar Enterprise: How the Alliance Revolution will Transform Global Business*. Perseus, 1998.

Fritzjof, Schuon. *Understanding Islam*. Penguin, 1972.

Ghoshal, Sumantra, and Christopher A. Bartlett. *The Individualised Corporation: Great Companies are Defined by Purpose, Process and People*. Heinemann, 1998.

Ghoshal, Sumantra, and Christopher A. Bartlett. *Managing Across Borders: The Transnational Solution*. Random House, 1998.

Gilad, Benjamin. *Business Blind Spots: Replacing Your Company's Entrenched and Outdated Myths, Beliefs and Assumptions with Today's Reality*. Probus, 1994.

Goleman, Daniel. *Emotional Intelligence*. Bloomsbury, 1995.

Gratton, Linda. *Living Strategy: Putting People at the Heart of Corporate Purpose*. Prentice Hall, 2000.

Greising, David. *I'd Like the World to Buy a Coke: The Life and Leadership of Roberto Goizueta*. John Wiley & Sons, 1998.

Hamel, Gary, and C.K. Prahalad. *Competing for the Future: Breakthrough Strategies for Seizing Control*. HBS Press, 1994.

Hammer, Michael. *Beyond Reengineering*. Harper Business, 1995.

Hammer, Michael, and James Champy. *Reengineering the Corporation: A Manifesto for Business Revolution*. Harper Business, 1994.

Hampden-Turner, Charles. *Creating Corporate Culture: From Discord to Harmony*. Addison Wesley, 1992.

Handy, Charles. *Understanding Organizations*. Penguin, 1976.

Handy, Charles. *The Empty Raincoat: Making Sense of the Future*. Arrow, 1995.

Hinsley, F.H. *Power and the Pursuit of Peace: Theory and Practice in the History of Relations Between States*. CUP, 1963.

Hobbes, Thomas. *The Leviathan*. Penguin, 1986.

Imai, Masaaki. *Kaizen*. Random House, 1986.

James, William. *The Varieties of Religious Experience*. Macmillan, 1961.

Kaplan, Robert S., and David P. Norton. *The Balanced Scorecard: Translating Strategy into Action*. HBS Press, 1996.

Kapleau, Philip. *The Three Pillars of Zen*. Anchor, 1989.

Katzenbach, Jon, and Douglas Smith. *The Wisdom of Teams*. HBS Press, 1993.

Kennedy, Paul. *The Rise and Fall of the Great Powers: Economic Change and Military Conflict from 1500 to 2000*. Fontana Press, 1988.

Kinsley, David. *Hinduism: A Cultural Perspective*. Prentice Hall, 1982.

Koch, Richard. *Moses on Leadership: Or Why Everyone is a Leader*. Capstone, 1999.

Kohn, Alfie. 'Why Incentive Plans Cannot Work.' *Harvard Business Review*, September/October 1993.

Kotter, John P. 'Leading Change: Why Transformation Efforts Fail.' *Harvard Business Review*, March/April 1995.

Kotter, John, and James Heskett. *Corporate Culture and Performance*. The Free Press, 1992.

Larkin, T.J. *Communicating Change*. McGraw-Hill, 1994.

Landes, David. *The Wealth and Poverty of Nations*. Abacus, 1998.

McIntosh, M., D. Leipziger, K. Jones, and J. Coleman. *Corporate Citizenship. Successful Strategies for Responsible Companies*. Pitman, 1998.

McKenna, Regis. *Real Time: Preparing for the Age of the Never Satisfied Customer*. HBS Press, 1997.

Merton, Thomas. *The Way to Chuang Tzu*. New Directions, 1965.

Mill, John Stuart. *On Liberty*. Penguin, 1974.

Mitchell, Stephen. *Tao Te Ching*. Harper & Row, 1989.

Mitroff, Ian. *A Spiritual Audit of Corporate America: A Hard Look at Spirituality, Religion and Values in the Workplace*. Jossey-Bass, 1999.

Mohrman, Susan Albers, Susan G. Cohen, and Allan M. Mohrman. *Designing Team-Based Organizations: New Forms of Knowledge Work*. Jossey-Bass, 1995.

Moore, James F. *The Death of Competition: Leadership and Strategy in the Age of Business Ecosystems*. John Wiley & Sons, 1996.

More, Thomas. *Utopia*. Penguin, 1965.

Negroponte, Nicholas. *Being Digital: The Road Map for Survival on the Information Superhighway*. Hodder & Stoughton, 1995.

Nonaka, Ikujiro, and Hirotaka Takeushi. *The Knowledge Creating Company: How Japanese Companies Create the Dynamics of Innovation*. OUP, 1995.

Ness, John B. *Man's Religions*. Macmillan, 1984.

Ohmae, Kenichi. *The Borderless World: Power and Strategy in the Interlinked Economy*. Harper Business, 1990.

Ohmae, Kenichi. *The End of the Nation State: The Rise of Regional Economies*. The Free Press, 1996.

Olins, Wally. *Corporate Identity: Making Business Strategy Visible through Design*. Thames & Hudson, 1994.

Olins, Wally. *Trading Identities: Why Countries and Companies are Taking on Each Other's Roles*. The Foreign Policy Centre, 1999.

Peters, Tom, and Robert Waterman. *In Search of Excellence*. Warner Books, 1988.

Porass, Jerry J., and James C. Collins. *Built to Last: Successful Habits of Visionary Companies*. Harper Business, 1994.

Porter, Michael E. *Competitive Strategy: Techniques for Analyzing Industries and Competitors*. The Free Press, 1980.

Porter, Michael E. *Competitive Advantage: Creating and Sustaining Superior Performance.* The Free Press, 1985.

Porter, Michael E. *The Competitive Advantage of Nations.* The Free Press, 1993.

Prahalad, C.K., and Gary Hamel. 'The Core Competencies of The Corporation.' *Harvard Business Review*, May/June 1990.

Pratt, J.B. *The Pilgrimage of Buddhism and a Buddhist Pilgrimage.* AMS Press, 1928.

Randall, William Sterne. *Thomas Jefferson: A Life.* Harper Perennial, 1993.

Rappaport, Alfred. *Creating Shareholder Value: A New Standard for Business.* The Free Press, 1986.

Risher, Howard, and Charles Fay. *The Performance Imperative: Strategies for Enhancing Workforce Effectiveness.* Jossey-Bass, 1995.

Robinson, Richard, and Will Johnston. *The Buddhist Religion.* Wadsworth, 1982.

Rousseau, Jean-Jacques. *The Social Contract.* Penguin, 1968.

Ruggles, Rudy L. *Knowledge Management Tools.* Butterworth Heinemann, 1997.

Schumacher, E.F. *A Guide for the Perplexed.* Harper and Row, 1976.

Scott, Mark C. *Value Drivers: The Manager's Guide to Driving Corporate Value Creation.* John Wiley & Sons, 1999.

Scott, Mark C. *The Professional Service Firm: A Manager's Guide to Maximising Profit and Value.* John Wiley & Sons, 2000.

Scott, Mark C. *Reinspiring the Corporation: The Seven Seminal Paths to Corporate Greatness.* John Wiley & Sons, 2000.

Seltzer, Robert M. *Jewish People, Jewish Thought.* Macmillan, 1980.

Smith, Huston. *The World's Religions.* HarperCollins, 1991.

Soros, George. *The Crisis of Global Capitalism: Open Society Endangered.* Little, Brown, 1998.

Stewart, Thomas A. *Intellectual Capital: The New Wealth of Organisations.* Nicholas Brealey Publishing, 1997.

Story, Jonathan. *The Frontiers of Fortune: Predicting Capital Prospects and Casualties in the Markets of the Future.* Prentice Hall, 1999.

Sveiby, Karl Erik. *The New Organizational Wealth, Managing and Measuring Knowledge Based Assets.* Berrett-Koehler, 1997.

Tomasko, Robert. *Downsizing: Reshaping the Corporation for the Future*. Amacom, 1987.

Waley, Arthur. *The Way and Its Power*. Allen & Unwin, 1958.

Zimmer, Heinrich. *The Philosophies of India*. Princeton University Press, 1969.

Index